thenewclassi

THE AUSTRALIAN
Women's Weekly

As times change, so do the dishes that turn up on our tables. The traditional Sunday lamb roast has given way to slow-cooked lamb shanks and, instead of a plain garden salad, a delicious spicy Thai beef salad may now grace the table. All we did was pick dishes that we love to eat today, and there was no shortage of things to choose from. It just goes to show that today's favourites can be tomorrow's classics.

Pamela Clark

Food Director

contents

Just a few short years ago many of the ingredients we now take for granted were either totally unknown or considered forebodingly foreign. When once we only had long-grain rice, we now have containers of jasmine, arborio and basmati close at hand to accompany the appropriate main course. Now mizuna and baby rocket nestle up to the iceberg in the vegie crisper, and there are bottles of kecap manis, mirin and fish sauce standing beside worcestershire, white vinegar and barbecue sauce on the shelf. Season with salt and pepper? Yes, of course ... but with sumac, ground ancho or cumin, too. As we've become increasingly multicultural and more aware of the delicious possibilities proffered by a hundred different nations' cuisines, we've adapted and adopted and adored them, making them our own new classics. Here are but a few of the many ingredients readily found at the local supermarket today.

star anise
vietnamese mint
kaffir lime
sumac
lemon grass
balsamic vinegar
za'atar
sichuan pepper
sambal oelek
kecap manis
fish sauce
baby vegetables
rocket
truss tomatoes
grape tomatoes
mirin
thai basil
baby bok choy
gai larn
haloumi
blood oranges
pomegranate
rice paper
different noodles
bavette pasta
figs

STARTERS

avocado caprese salad

PREPARATION TIME 10 MINUTES

4 large vine-ripened
tomatoes (480g)

250g cherry bocconcini

1 large avocado (320g), halved

¼ cup loosely packed fresh
basil leaves

2 tablespoons olive oil

1 tablespoon balsamic vinegar

1 Slice tomato, cheese and avocado thickly.
2 Place slices of tomato, cheese and avocado on serving platter;
   top with basil leaves, drizzle with combined oil and vinegar.
   Sprinkle with freshly ground black pepper, if desired.

serves 4
per serving 29g total fat (10.1g saturated fat); 1342kJ
(321 cal); 2.3g carbohydrate; 13.1g protein; 2.3g fibre

TIP *We used vine-ripened
truss tomatoes because it
takes a simple recipe like
this for their brilliant
colour, robust flavour and
crisp, tangy flesh to stand
out at their magnificent
best. Use less costly
tomatoes to cook with, but
always go for these when
you're serving them raw.*

tom yum goong

PREPARATION TIME 30 MINUTES **COOKING TIME** 20 MINUTES

1 Place stock, coriander root and stem mixture, lemon grass, lime leaves, ginger, chilli and sauce in large saucepan; bring to a boil. Reduce heat; simmer, uncovered, 10 minutes.
2 Meanwhile, shell and devein prawns, leaving tails intact.
3 Add prawns, onion and juice to pan; simmer, uncovered, about 4 minutes or until prawns just change in colour. Remove from heat; stir in coriander and basil leaves.

serves 4
per serving 1.6g total fat (0.5g saturated fat); 602kJ (114 cal); 4.4g carbohydrate; 27g protein; 1.4g fibre

1.5 litres (6 cups) fish stock

1 tablespoon coarsely chopped coriander root and stem mixture

10cm stick (20g) thinly sliced fresh lemon grass

8 fresh kaffir lime leaves, torn

8cm piece fresh ginger (40g), sliced thinly

2 fresh small red thai chillies, sliced thinly

1 tablespoon fish sauce

12 uncooked large king prawns (840g)

8 green onions, cut into 2cm lengths

⅓ cup (80ml) lime juice

⅔ cup loosely packed fresh coriander leaves

½ cup loosely packed fresh thai basil leaves, torn

TIP *After removing the leaves, wash the stems and roots from the coriander really well then chop some of them for this recipe. You can freeze chopped roots and stems, if you like, wrapped tightly in plastic.*

TIP *You'll need three juicy limes for this recipe.*

TIP *Garlic's cooking times make a huge difference to its pungency: the longer it's cooked, the more creamy in texture and subtly nutty in flavour it becomes. This soup and the French classic, Chicken with Forty Cloves of Garlic, are delicious culinary proof that more can be less, depending on the cooking process.*

2 medium garlic bulbs (140g), unpeeled

2 tablespoons olive oil

2 medium brown onions (300g), chopped coarsely

1 tablespoon fresh thyme leaves

5 medium potatoes (1kg), chopped coarsely

1.25 litres (5 cups) chicken stock

¾ cup (180ml) cream

cream of roasted garlic and potato soup

PREPARATION TIME 10 MINUTES **COOKING TIME** 30 MINUTES

1 Preheat oven to moderate.
2 Separate garlic bulbs into cloves; place unpeeled cloves, in single layer, on oven tray. Drizzle with half of the oil. Roast, uncovered, in moderate oven about 15 minutes or until garlic is soft. Remove from oven; when cool enough to handle, squeeze garlic into small bowl, discard skins.
3 Meanwhile, heat remaining oil in large saucepan; cook onion and thyme, stirring, until onion softens. Add potato; cook, stirring, 5 minutes. Add stock; bring to a boil. Reduce heat; simmer, uncovered, about 15 minutes or until potato is just tender. Stir in garlic; simmer, uncovered, 5 minutes.
4 Blend or process soup (or pass through a food mill [mouli] or fine sieve), in batches, until smooth then return to pan. Reheat until hot then stir in cream. Divide soup among serving bowls; sprinkle with extra thyme, if desired.

serves 4
per serving 27.9g total fat (13g saturated fat); 1864kJ (446 cal); 36.8g carbohydrate; 12g protein; 8.5g fibre

TIP *You can double or treble this aïoli recipe, if you like, but don't throw the egg whites away... freeze them until you have enough to make a pavlova or friands. If the aïoli you've made separates, place a yolk in another bowl and whisk the separated aïoli into it. The added yolk will re-emulsify the sauce.*

salt and pepper baby octopus with aïoli

PREPARATION TIME 15 MINUTES **COOKING TIME** 5 MINUTES

1 Make aïoli.
2 Combine octopus, salt and pepper in medium bowl.
3 Place ingredients for dressing in screw-top jar; shake well.
4 Place mesclun, cucumber, tomato and dressing in large bowl; toss gently to combine.
5 Heat oil in wok; stir-fry octopus, in batches, until browned lightly and cooked through.
6 Serve octopus on salad with aïoli and lemon wedges, if desired.

AÏOLI Blend or process egg yolk, garlic, mustard and vinegar until combined. With motor operating, gradually add oil in thin, steady stream; process until aïoli thickens slightly. Stir in juice.

serves 4
per serving 74.3g total fat (10.9g saturated fat); 3348kJ (801 cal); 3.5g carbohydrate; 31.4g protein; 2.1g fibre

500g cleaned baby octopus, halved lengthways

2 teaspoons sea salt

3 teaspoons cracked black pepper

150g mesclun

1 lebanese cucumber (130g), sliced thinly

125g cherry tomatoes, halved

2 tablespoons olive oil

AÏOLI

1 egg yolk

1 clove garlic, crushed

1 teaspoon dijon mustard

1 tablespoon white wine vinegar

1 cup (250ml) olive oil

1 teaspoon lemon juice

DRESSING

1 tablespoon lemon juice

1 tablespoon olive oil

PIZZETTA 3WAYS

Our basic pizza dough recipe will make four pizzetta bases. Each of the following topping recipes is enough for four pizzetta bases. Increase the quantities of pizza dough you prepare proportionately to the number of different toppings you want to make.

basic pizza dough

PREPARATION TIME 15 MINUTES (PLUS STANDING TIME)

1 cup (250ml) warm water

1 teaspoon caster sugar

2 teaspoons (7g) dried yeast

2½ cups (375g) plain flour

1 teaspoon salt

1 Combine the water, sugar and yeast in small jug; stand in warm place about 10 minutes or until mixture is frothy.
2 Combine yeast mixture with flour and salt in large bowl, using hand to mix well. Turn dough onto lightly floured surface; knead about 10 minutes or until smooth and elastic.
3 Place dough in large oiled bowl; stand in warm place, covered, about 1 hour or until dough doubles in size.
4 Meanwhile, while dough is standing, make the topping of your choice from the three shown here, following directions in that particular recipe to finish the pizzetta.

per serving 1.2g total fat (0.2g saturated fat); 1396kJ (334 cal); 68.7g carbohydrate; 10.8g protein; 4g fibre

TIP *The basic dough can also be rolled out to make a single large pizza base, if you prefer.*

TIP *Pizzetta can be cooked on pizza trays, uncovered, in a preheated very hot oven for about 15 minutes or until the crust is browned and crisp as desired.*

TIP *Invite your friends over for a DIY-pizzetta barbie! Prepare our suggested toppings and set them out in separate bowls. When the grill and your guests are ready to go, pass the half-browned bases on foil-lined plates and let your pals choose their own toppings. Slide the bases back onto the bbq, cover the pizzetta and hand the job (and the tongs) over to the assembled throng to complete.*

onion, anchovy and olive pizzetta

PREPARATION TIME 15 MINUTES **COOKING TIME** 20 MINUTES

1 Heat oil in large frying pan; cook onion, stirring, until browned lightly. Add sherry; cook, stirring, until sherry evaporates.
2 Preheat barbecue or grill plate to medium heat.
3 Divide dough into four portions; roll each portion to form 15cm-round pizzetta base. Cover barbecue grill plate with double thickness of oiled foil. Place pizzetta bases on foil; cook, uncovered, 5 minutes.
4 Using metal tongs, turn bases; spread cooked sides with tomato paste. Divide onion mixture among pizzetta; top with anchovies, olives and oregano. Cook, covered, over low heat about 5 minutes or until bases are cooked through.

per serving 6.8g total fat (1g saturated fat); 1835kJ (439 cal); 76g carbohydrate; 14.9g protein; 5.9g fibre

1 tablespoon olive oil

3 medium brown onions (450g), sliced thinly

2 tablespoons dry sherry

2 tablespoons tomato paste

12 drained anchovy fillets, chopped coarsely

¼ cup (40g) thinly sliced seeded kalamata olives

2 tablespoons fresh oregano leaves

TIP *It's easy to make pesto from different herbs or green leaves and with other nuts. One of our favourite combos is baby rocket and pistachio (it goes beautifully with chicken). A few other enticing blends include fresh coriander leaves with chilli instead of nuts, and sun-dried tomatoes processed with olives and walnuts. Mix and match ingredients until you find a flavourful paste you like best.*

semi-dried tomato, basil pesto and ricotta pizzetta

PREPARATION TIME 20 MINUTES **COOKING TIME** 10 MINUTES

1 cup firmly packed fresh basil leaves

1 tablespoon pine nuts

1 clove garlic, quartered

¼ cup (20g) coarsely grated parmesan cheese

¼ cup (60ml) olive oil

1 fresh long red chilli, sliced thinly

1 cup (200g) ricotta cheese

½ cup (75g) drained semi-dried tomatoes

⅓ cup loosely packed fresh small basil leaves, extra

1 Blend or process basil, nuts, garlic, parmesan and oil until pesto forms a smooth paste.
2 Preheat barbecue or grill plate to medium heat.
3 Divide dough into four portions; roll each portion to form 15cm-round pizzetta base. Cover barbecue grill plate with double thickness of oiled foil. Place pizzetta bases on foil; cook, uncovered, 5 minutes.
4 Using metal tongs, turn bases; spread cooked sides with pesto. Divide chilli, ricotta and tomato among bases. Cook, covered, over low heat about 5 minutes or until bases are cooked through; sprinkle with extra basil.

per serving 26.2g total fat (7.1g saturated fat); 2617kJ (626 cal); 76.2g carbohydrate; 20.7g protein; 7.3g fibre

TIP *Be sure to invest in a really good quality but simple tomato pasta sauce for any pizzetta or pizza topping. Cheap generic varieties won't do the taste of the finished pizza any favours, especially if they're laden with overpowering dried herbs or other flavour enhancers. Remember that the unused portion of the sauce will keep for a few weeks, tightly sealed, in the refrigerator.*

fig, prosciutto and goat cheese pizzetta

PREPARATION TIME 10 MINUTES **COOKING TIME** 10 MINUTES

1 Preheat barbecue or grill plate to medium heat.
2 Divide dough into four portions; roll each portion to form 15cm-round pizzetta base. Cover barbecue grill plate with double thickness of oiled foil. Place pizzetta bases on foil; cook, uncovered, 5 minutes.
3 Using metal tongs, turn bases; spread cooked side with pasta sauce. Divide cheese, fig and prosciutto among bases. Cook, covered, over low heat about 5 minutes or until bases are cooked through; top with rocket.

per serving 6.4g total fat (3.1g saturated fat); 1797kJ (430 cal); 74.4g carbohydrate; 17.8g protein; 5.4g fibre

⅓ cup (85g) bottled tomato pasta sauce

100g goat cheese, crumbled

2 large figs (160g), cut into thin wedges

4 slices prosciutto (60g), chopped coarsely

25g baby rocket leaves

tuna tartare with avocado salsa and parmesan crisps

PREPARATION TIME 40 MINUTES **COOKING TIME** 5 MINUTES

1 cup (80g) coarsely grated parmesan cheese

½ fresh long red chilli, sliced thinly

400g piece sashimi tuna, trimmed

1 small avocado (200g), chopped finely

3 small tomatoes (270g), seeded, chopped finely

1 small red onion (100g), chopped finely

⅓ cup loosely packed fresh coriander leaves

CHILLI LIME DRESSING

½ fresh long red chilli, sliced thinly

1 teaspoon finely grated lime rind

⅓ cup (80ml) lime juice

1 clove garlic, crushed

2 teaspoons finely chopped coriander root and stem mixture

2 tablespoons olive oil

1 Preheat oven to hot.

2 Combine cheese and chilli in small bowl. Drop level tablespoons of the cheese mixture on baking-paper-lined oven tray, flattening slightly with back of spoon. Bake, uncovered, in hot oven about 5 minutes or until browned lightly. Remove from oven; stand until parmesan crisps set.

3 Meanwhile, place ingredients for chilli lime dressing in screw-top jar; shake well.

4 Cut tuna into 5mm pieces. Place in medium bowl with half of the dressing; toss gently to combine.

5 Place avocado, tomato, onion and coriander in medium bowl with remaining dressing; toss gently to combine salsa.

6 Press a quarter of the undrained tuna into a 9cm egg ring set on serving plate; remove egg ring, top tuna with a quarter of the salsa. Repeat with remaining tuna and salsa; serve tartare with parmesan crisps.

serves 4
per serving 29.4g total fat (9.4g saturated fat); 1731kJ (414 cal); 2.6g carbohydrate; 34.6g protein; 2g fibre

TIP *Tuna sold as sashimi has to meet stringent guidelines regarding its handling and treatment after leaving the water. Regardless, it is still probably a good idea to know your fishmonger quite well or to seek advice from local authorities before eating any raw seafood.*

chinese wonton soup

PREPARATION TIME 40 MINUTES
COOKING TIME 2 HOURS 10 MINUTES

Use crisp and crunchy fresh water chestnuts for this recipe if you can find them. Locally grown ones are sold in Asian food shops and some greengrocers in some months of the year.

Uncooked wontons can be frozen until required; cook, straight from the freezer, in the broth.

1 Combine bones, onion, carrot, the water, three-quarters of the ginger and half of the chilli in large saucepan; bring to a boil. Reduce heat; simmer, uncovered, about 2 hours or until reduced by half. Strain broth through muslin-lined sieve or colander into large bowl; discard solids. (Broth can be made ahead to this stage. Cover; refrigerate overnight or freeze.)

2 Meanwhile, chop remaining chilli finely. Combine in small bowl with pork, garlic, onion, water chestnut, coriander, oil, 2 teaspoons of the wine, 1 teaspoon of the soy sauce, half of the sugar and remaining ginger.

3 Place 1 level tablespoon of pork filling on centre of each wonton wrapper; brush around edges with a little water, gather edges around filling, pinch together to seal. Repeat process with remaining pork filling and wonton wrappers.

4 Skim fat from surface of broth; return broth to large saucepan. Add remaining wine, remaining soy sauce and remaining sugar; bring to a boil. Add wontons to pan; cook, uncovered, about 5 minutes or until cooked through.

5 Meanwhile, divide watercress and mushrooms among serving bowls. Using slotted spoon, transfer wontons from pan to bowls then ladle broth into bowls.

serves 4
per serving 4.4g total fat (1.3g saturated fat); 648kJ (155 cal); 16.2g carbohydrate; 11.2g protein; 2.7g fibre

1kg chicken bones

1 small brown onion (80g), quartered

1 medium carrot (120g), quartered

3 litres (12 cups) water

4cm piece fresh ginger (20g), grated

2 fresh small red thai chillies, halved lengthways

150g pork mince

1 clove garlic, crushed

1 green onion, chopped finely

2 tablespoons finely chopped water chestnuts

2 tablespoons finely chopped fresh coriander

1 teaspoon sesame oil

2 tablespoons chinese cooking wine

¼ cup (60ml) soy sauce

2 teaspoons caster sugar

12 wonton wrappers

1 cup firmly packed watercress sprigs

4 fresh shiitake mushrooms, sliced thinly

TIP *Wine is stirred into a risotto both to enhance flavour and to impart depth to the finished dish. Add it before the stock so that the alcohol burns off when the wine hits the base of the pan. A clean, dry white wine is best, although some cooks like red wine risottos. Finish the bottle of chilled wine with dinner.*

white wine risotto cakes with smoked chicken

PREPARATION TIME 20 MINUTES
COOKING TIME 45 MINUTES (PLUS COOLING AND REFRIGERATION TIME)

2¾ cups (680ml) chicken stock

10g butter

1 tablespoon olive oil

1 small brown onion (80g), chopped finely

1 clove garlic, crushed

⅔ cup (130g) arborio rice

¼ cup (60ml) dry white wine

¼ cup (20g) coarsely grated parmesan cheese

2 tablespoons finely shredded fresh basil

1 tablespoon dijon mustard

1 tablespoon sour cream

2 tablespoons vegetable oil

32 baby rocket leaves

170g smoked chicken breast, shredded coarsely

1 Place stock in medium saucepan; bring to a boil. Reduce heat; simmer, covered.

2 Meanwhile, heat butter and half of the olive oil in medium saucepan; cook onion and garlic, stirring, until onion just softens. Add rice; stir rice to coat in onion mixture. Add wine; cook, stirring, until wine is almost evaporated. Stir in ½ cup simmering stock; cook, stirring, over low heat until liquid is absorbed. Continue adding stock, in ½-cup batches, stirring until liquid is absorbed after each addition. Total cooking time should be about 30 minutes or until rice is tender. Gently stir in cheese and basil; cool 20 minutes.

3 Divide risotto into four portions; using hands, shape portions into 1cm-deep patty-shaped cakes. Refrigerate, covered, 30 minutes.

4 Meanwhile, combine mustard and sour cream in small bowl.

5 Heat vegetable oil in large frying pan; cook risotto cakes, uncovered, until browned both sides and heated through.

6 Place each risotto cake on serving plate; top each with 8 rocket leaves, a quarter of the chicken then 2 teaspoons of the mustard mixture; drizzle with remaining olive oil.

serves 4
per serving 23.4g total fat (6.7g saturated fat); 1676kJ (401 cal); 28.4g carbohydrate; 17.4g protein; 1g fibre

VIETNAMESE SUMMER ROLLS 4WAYS

Unlike traditional spring rolls, these classic Vietnamese rice paper rolls are served cold, a fresh alternative to the deep-fried variety. The chewy texture of the rice paper is nicely complemented by the crisp vegetables within. Each of these recipes makes 12 rolls.

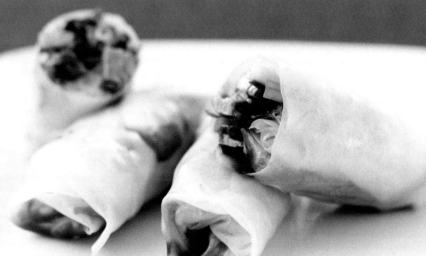

peking duck rolls

PREPARATION TIME 20 MINUTES

½ chinese barbecued duck

2 green onions

12 x 17cm-square rice paper sheets

2 tablespoons hoisin sauce

1 tablespoon plum sauce

1 lebanese cucumber (130g), seeded, cut into batons

1 Remove skin and meat from duck. Discard bones; slice meat and skin thinly. Cut each onion crossways into three equal pieces; slice pieces thinly lengthways.
2 To assemble rolls, place 1 sheet of rice paper in medium bowl of warm water until just softened. Lift sheet from water carefully; place, with one point of the square sheet facing you, on board covered with tea towel. Spread 1 teaspoon of combined hoisin and plum sauces vertically along centre of sheet; top with a little of the cucumber, a little of the green onion and a little of the duck meat. Fold top and bottom corners over filling then roll sheet from side to side to enclose filling. Repeat with remaining rice paper sheets, combined sauces, cucumber, onion and duck.

per serving 6g total fat (2.5g saturated fat); 472kJ (113 cal); 11.9g carbohydrate; 3.5g protein; 2.1g fibre

TIP *There are two different kinds of rice paper so, in this recipe, be sure you use the Vietnamese "banh trang", made from rice paste and stamped into squares or rounds that can be eaten without being cooked. The other, a glossy rice paper that's produced in Holland from a shrub, cannot be eaten uncooked, and is used in confectionery making and baking.*

coconut chicken rolls

PREPARATION TIME 20 MINUTES **COOKING TIME** 10 MINUTES

1 Combine chicken, coconut cream, stock, lemon grass, ginger and coriander root and stem mixture in medium saucepan; bring to a boil. Reduce heat; simmer, uncovered, about 5 minutes or until chicken is cooked through. Cool chicken in poaching liquid 10 minutes. Remove chicken from pan; reserve ¼ cup of the poaching liquid, discard remainder.
2 Chop chicken finely; place in medium bowl with snow peas, coriander and poaching liquid, toss gently to combine.
3 To assemble rolls, place 1 sheet of rice paper in medium bowl of warm water until just softened. Lift sheet from water carefully; place, with one point of the square sheet facing you, on board covered with tea towel. Place a little of the chicken filling vertically along centre of sheet; fold top and bottom corners over filling then roll sheet from side to side to enclose filling. Repeat with remaining rice paper sheets and chicken filling.
4 Combine dipping sauce ingredients in small bowl; serve with rolls.

per serving 3g total fat (2.1g saturated fat); 309kJ (74 cal); 5g carbohydrate; 6.9g protein; 0.7g fibre

300g chicken tenderloins

½ cup (125ml) coconut cream

½ cup (125ml) chicken stock

10cm stick (20g) coarsely chopped fresh lemon grass

5cm piece fresh ginger (25g), grated

1 tablespoon coarsely chopped coriander root and stem mixture

100g snow peas, trimmed, sliced thinly

½ cup coarsely chopped fresh coriander

12 x 17cm-square rice paper sheets

SWEET CHILLI DIPPING SAUCE

¼ cup (60ml) sweet chilli sauce

1 tablespoon fish sauce

1 tablespoon lime juice

TIP *Rice vermicelli, also known as "bee hoon", is used throughout South-East Asia in soups, salads, rolls and stir-fries. It is similar to bean thread noodles, which are made from mung bean starch instead of rice flour. Both can be deep-fried or simply softened in very hot water to make them ready to eat. Bean thread noodles and rice vermicelli can be substituted for one another, and thin rice stick noodles for either.*

noodle and vegetable rolls

PREPARATION TIME 20 MINUTES **COOKING TIME** 5 MINUTES

60g rice vermicelli

½ medium carrot (60g), grated coarsely

½ small chinese cabbage (350g), shredded finely

1 tablespoon fish sauce

1 tablespoon brown sugar

¼ cup (60ml) lemon juice

12 x 17cm-square rice paper sheets

12 large fresh mint leaves

SWEET CHILLI DIPPING SAUCE

¼ cup (60ml) sweet chilli sauce

1 tablespoon fish sauce

1 tablespoon lime juice

1 Place noodles in medium heatproof bowl, cover with boiling water; stand until just tender, drain. Using kitchen scissors, cut noodles into random lengths.
2 Place noodles in medium bowl with carrot, cabbage, fish sauce, sugar and juice; toss gently to combine.
3 To assemble rolls, place 1 sheet of rice paper in medium bowl of warm water until just softened. Lift sheet from water carefully; place, with one point of the square sheet facing you, on board covered with tea towel. Place a little of the vegetable filling and one mint leaf vertically along centre of sheet; fold top and bottom corners over filling then roll sheet from side to side to enclose filling. Repeat with remaining rice paper sheets, vegetable filling and mint leaves.
4 Combine ingredients for sweet chilli dipping sauce in small bowl; serve with rolls.

per serving 0.2g total fat (0g saturated fat); 188kJ (45 cal); 9g carbohydrate; 1.4g protein; 0.8g fibre

TIP *The number of filling and dipping sauce possibilities you can make depends on how imaginative you are. Think outside the square: come up with seasonal variations; choose ingredients that are not particularly Asian; or use them as a vehicle for leftovers.*

TIP *Pour hot water into a bowl larger than the rice paper so it can be immersed all at once.*

pork and prawn rolls

PREPARATION TIME 35 MINUTES **COOKING TIME** 50 MINUTES

1 Cover pork with water in medium saucepan, cover; bring to a boil. Reduce heat; simmer, uncovered, about 45 minutes or until pork is tender. Drain; when cool enough to handle, slice thinly.
2 Meanwhile, shell and devein prawns; chop prawn meat finely. Make hoisin and peanut dipping sauce. Combine lettuce, sprouts and mint in medium bowl.
3 To assemble rolls, place 1 sheet of rice paper in medium bowl of warm water until just softened. Lift sheet from water carefully; place, with one point of the square sheet facing you, on board covered with tea towel. Place a little of the prawn meat vertically along centre of sheet; top with a little of the pork then a little of the lettuce filling. Fold top and bottom corners over filling then roll sheet from side to side to enclose filling. Repeat with remaining rice paper sheets, prawn meat, pork and lettuce filling.

HOISIN AND PEANUT DIPPING SAUCE Combine sugar, vinegar and the water in small saucepan; stir over medium heat until sugar dissolves. Stir in sauce and nuts. Serve with rolls.

per serving 2g total fat (0.5g saturated fat); 355kJ (85 cal); 5.4g carbohydrate; 11g protein; 1.2g fibre

200g pork belly

650g cooked medium king prawns

1⅓ cups (80g) finely shredded iceberg lettuce

1 cup (80g) bean sprouts

½ cup loosely packed fresh mint leaves

12 x 17cm-square rice paper sheets

HOISIN AND PEANUT DIPPING SAUCE

2 teaspoons caster sugar

1 tablespoon rice vinegar

¼ cup (60ml) water

¼ cup (60ml) hoisin sauce

1 tablespoon crushed toasted peanuts

LIGHT MEALS

penne with char-grilled capsicum and pine nuts

PREPARATION TIME 15 MINUTES **COOKING TIME** 20 MINUTES

2 large red capsicums (700g)

375g penne

2 tablespoons olive oil

2 cloves garlic, crushed

½ cup (80g) toasted pine nuts

2 fresh small red thai chillies, chopped finely

¼ cup (60ml) lemon juice

100g baby rocket leaves

100g fetta cheese, crumbled

1 Quarter capsicums; discard seeds and membranes. Roast under grill or in very hot oven, skin-side up, until skin blisters and blackens. Cover capsicum pieces in plastic or paper for 5 minutes, peel away skin then slice thinly.
2 Cook pasta in large saucepan of boiling water, uncovered, until just tender; drain.
3 Meanwhile, heat oil in large frying pan; cook garlic, nuts and chilli, stirring, about 2 minutes or until fragrant. Add capsicum and juice; stir until hot.
4 Place pasta and capsicum mixture in large bowl with rocket and cheese; toss gently to combine.

serves 4
per serving 30.5g total fat (6.2g saturated fat); 2755kJ (659 cal); 74.4g carbohydrate; 21g protein; 8.2g fibre

TIP *A few hours spent in the kitchen on Sunday will go a long way towards simplifying a weeknight meal like this. Char-grill and peel several capsicums at one time then store the roasted sliced flesh, covered with olive oil in a tightly sealed glass jar and refrigerated, taking out only as much as you need for any given recipe.*

chicken laksa

PREPARATION TIME 30 MINUTES (PLUS COOLING TIME)
COOKING TIME 45 MINUTES

1 Place the water in large saucepan; bring to a boil. Add 4 lime leaves, garlic and chicken, reduce heat; simmer, covered, about 15 minutes or until chicken is cooked through. Cool chicken in liquid 15 minutes. Slice chicken thinly; reserve. Strain stock through muslin-lined sieve or colander into large bowl; discard solids. Allow stock to cool; skim fat from surface.

2 Cook laksa paste in large saucepan, stirring, until fragrant. Stir in stock, coconut milk, chilli and remaining torn lime leaves; bring to a boil. Reduce heat; simmer, uncovered, 20 minutes.

3 Meanwhile, place rice stick noodles in large heatproof bowl, cover with boiling water, stand until just tender; drain. Place singapore noodles in separate large heatproof bowl; cover with boiling water, separate with fork, drain. Divide both noodles among serving bowls.

4 Stir sugar, juice, sauce, tofu and chicken into laksa. Ladle laksa over noodles; sprinkle with combined sprouts and herbs.

serves 4
per serving 69.7g total fat (42.2g saturated fat); 4577kJ (1095 cal); 65g carbohydrate; 53.2g protein; 10.8g fibre

1 litre (4 cups) water

12 fresh kaffir lime leaves

2 cloves garlic, quartered

800g chicken thigh fillets

½ cup (150g) laksa paste

3¼ cups (800ml) coconut milk

2 fresh red thai chillies, chopped finely

150g dried rice stick noodles

175g singapore noodles

2 tablespoons grated palm sugar

⅓ cup (80ml) lime juice

2 tablespoons fish sauce

80g fried tofu puffs, halved

1½ cups (120g) bean sprouts

½ cup loosely packed fresh coriander leaves

½ cup loosely packed fresh vietnamese mint leaves

TIP Commercial laksa pastes vary dramatically in their heat intensity so, while we call for ½ cup here, you might try using less of the laksa paste you've purchased until you can determine how hot it makes the final dish.

caesar salad

PREPARATION TIME 30 MINUTES **COOKING TIME** 20 MINUTES

Named after Caesar Cardini, the Italian-American who tossed the first Caesar in his restaurant in Tijuana, Mexico, during the 1920s, this salad must always contain – as authenticated by Cardini's daughter – freshly made garlic croutons, crisp cos lettuce leaves, coddled eggs, lemon juice, olive oil, Worcestershire sauce, black pepper and parmesan... no single ingredient is meant to dominate. The original Caesar didn't contain bacon, hard-boiled egg, chicken breast or anchovies (the Worcestershire gave it that anchovy flavour).

½ loaf ciabatta (220g)

1 clove garlic, crushed

⅓ cup (80ml) olive oil

2 eggs

3 baby cos lettuces (540g), leaves separated

1 cup (80g) flaked parmesan cheese

CAESAR DRESSING

1 clove garlic, crushed

1 tablespoon dijon mustard

2 tablespoons lemon juice

2 teaspoons worcestershire sauce

2 tablespoons olive oil

1 Preheat oven to moderate.
2 Cut bread into 2cm cubes. Combine garlic and oil in large bowl, add bread; toss bread to coat in oil mixture. Place bread, in single layer, on oven trays; toast, uncovered, in moderate oven about 15 minutes or until croutons are browned lightly.
3 Bring water to a boil in small saucepan; using slotted spoon, carefully lower whole eggs into water. Cover pan tightly, remove from heat; using same slotted spoon, remove eggs from water after 1 minute. When cool enough to handle, break eggs into large bowl, add lettuce; toss gently to combine. Add cheese and croutons.
4 Place ingredients for caesar dressing in screw-top jar; shake well. Pour dressing over salad; toss gently to combine. Divide among serving plates; sprinkle with freshly ground black pepper, if desired.

serves 4
per serving 38.4g total fat (9g saturated fat); 2195kJ (525 cal); 28g carbohydrate; 17.7g protein; 4.6g fibre

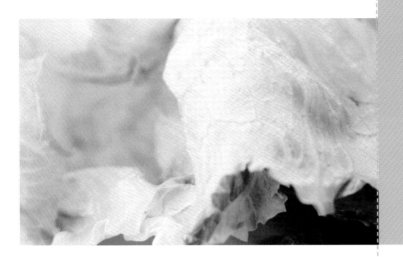

TIP *An easy way to remove whole lettuce leaves is to rap the head, stem-end down, on a hard surface to loosen the core. Discard the core, and run a strong stream of cold water into the cavity - the leaves will fall away, intact. Submerge the leaves in iced water until ready to serve; use the lettuce centre for a salad.*

pork and chicken
sang choy bow

PREPARATION TIME 20 MINUTES **COOKING TIME** 45 MINUTES

1 Preheat oven to moderate.
2 Place pork on wire rack in large shallow baking dish; brush all over with ¼ cup of the char siu sauce. Roast, uncovered, in moderate oven about 40 minutes or until cooked as desired, brushing occasionally with pan drippings. Cool 10 minutes; chop pork finely.
3 Meanwhile, heat peanut oil in wok; stir-fry chicken, garlic and mushrooms, 5 minutes. Add water chestnuts, chopped onion, sauces, sesame oil, pork and remaining char siu sauce; stir-fry until chicken is cooked through. Remove from heat; add sprouts, toss sang choy bow gently to combine.
4 Divide lettuce leaves among serving plates; spoon sang choy bow into leaves, sprinkle each with sliced onion.

serves 4
per serving 13.4g total fat (3.1g saturated fat); 1430kJ (342 cal); 17.5g carbohydrate; 37.9g protein; 6.1g fibre

500g pork fillets

⅓ cup (80ml) char siu sauce

1 tablespoon peanut oil

150g chicken mince

1 clove garlic, crushed

100g fresh shiitake mushrooms, chopped finely

190g can water chestnuts, rinsed, drained, chopped finely

2 green onions, chopped finely

2 tablespoons oyster sauce

1 tablespoon soy sauce

1 teaspoon sesame oil

1½ cups (120g) bean sprouts

8 large iceberg lettuce leaves

2 green onions, sliced thinly

BARBECUED DUCK 2WAYS

How easy is this? Buy a succulent barbecued duck on the way home, shred the meat then toss it in a bowl with the ingredients from either one of these great salad ideas. Each of the recipes here makes a large enough salad to serve four.

asian duck salad

PREPARATION TIME 25 MINUTES

1kg chinese barbecued duck

150g snow peas, trimmed, sliced thinly

1 green mango (350g), sliced thinly

3 shallots (75g), sliced thinly

125g mizuna

⅓ cup firmly packed fresh mint leaves

⅓ cup firmly packed fresh coriander leaves

1 fresh long red chilli, sliced thinly

THAI DRESSING

2 tablespoons fish sauce

2 tablespoons grated palm sugar

⅓ cup (80ml) lime juice

2 teaspoons peanut oil

1 Remove meat, leaving skin on, from duck; discard bones. Chop meat coarsely; place in large bowl with remaining ingredients.
2 Place ingredients for thai dressing in screw-top jar; shake well. Pour over salad; toss gently to combine.

per serving 35.2g total fat (10g saturated fat); 2082kJ (498 cal); 17.8g carbohydrate; 28.1g protein; 3.3g fibre

duck salad with mandarin and pomegranate

PREPARATION TIME 25 MINUTES **COOKING TIME** 5 MINUTES

You need one large pomegranate for this recipe.

1 Boil, steam or microwave peas until just tender; drain. Rinse under cold water; drain.
2 Remove meat, leaving skin on, from duck; discard bones. Chop meat coarsely; place in large bowl with peas, mandarin, lettuce, pomegranate and nuts.
3 Place ingredients for lemon dijon dressing in screw-top jar; shake well. Pour dressing over salad; toss gently to combine.

per serving 58.3g total fat (12.7g saturated fat); 2876kJ (688 cal); 8.9g carbohydrate; 33.3g protein; 6.5g fibre

150g sugar snap peas, trimmed

1kg chinese barbecued duck

2 small mandarins (200g), segmented

1 red mignonette lettuce (280g)

⅓ cup (60g) pomegranate pulp

¾ cup (120g) toasted slivered almonds

LEMON DIJON DRESSING

1 clove garlic, crushed

1 teaspoon dijon mustard

2 tablespoons lemon juice

2 tablespoons olive oil

vietnamese chicken salad

PREPARATION TIME 20 MINUTES **COOKING TIME** 15 MINUTES

500g chicken breast fillets

1 large carrot (180g)

½ cup (125ml) rice wine vinegar

2 teaspoons salt

2 tablespoons caster sugar

1 medium white onion (150g), sliced thinly

1½ cups (120g) bean sprouts

2 cups (160g) finely shredded savoy cabbage

¼ cup firmly packed fresh vietnamese mint leaves

½ cup firmly packed fresh coriander leaves

1 tablespoon crushed toasted peanuts

2 tablespoons fried shallots

VIETNAMESE DRESSING

2 tablespoons fish sauce

¼ cup (60ml) water

2 tablespoons caster sugar

2 tablespoons lime juice

1 clove garlic, crushed

1 Place chicken in medium saucepan of boiling water; return to a boil. Reduce heat; simmer, uncovered, about 10 minutes or until cooked through. Cool chicken in poaching liquid 10 minutes; discard liquid (or reserve for another use). Shred chicken coarsely.

2 Meanwhile, cut carrot into matchstick-sized pieces. Combine carrot in large bowl with vinegar, salt and sugar, cover; stand 5 minutes. Add onion, cover; stand 5 minutes. Add sprouts, cover; stand 3 minutes. Drain pickled vegetables; discard liquid.

3 Place pickled vegetables in large bowl with chicken, cabbage, mint and coriander.

4 Place ingredients for vietnamese dressing in screw-top jar; shake well. Pour dressing over salad in bowl; toss gently to combine. Sprinkle with nuts and shallots.

serves 4
per serving 8.9g total fat (2.3g saturated fat); 1271kJ (304 cal); 24.3g carbohydrate; 31g protein; 5.1g fibre

TIP *Fried shallots, served as a condiment at Asian mealtimes or sprinkled over just-cooked food, provide an extra crunchy finish to a salad, stir-fry or curry. They can be purchased at all Asian grocery stores; once opened, they will keep for months if stored in a tightly sealed glass jar.*

slow-roasted mushrooms with creamy polenta

PREPARATION TIME 20 MINUTES (PLUS STANDING TIME)
COOKING TIME 40 MINUTES

1 Preheat oven to slow.
2 Combine oyster, shiitake, swiss brown and flat mushrooms, tomato, onion, garlic and oil in large baking dish; roast, uncovered, in slow oven about 30 minutes or until mushrooms are tender.
3 Meanwhile, soak porcini in the boiling water in small jug for 15 minutes. Drain over small bowl; reserve liquid. Chop porcini finely.
4 Combine reserved liquid, milk and the cold water in medium saucepan; bring to a boil. Gradually add polenta to pan, stirring. Reduce heat; cook, stirring, about 5 minutes or until polenta thickens slightly. Stir in porcini, butter and cheese.
5 Stir herbs into mushroom mixture. Divide polenta among serving plates; top with mushroom mixture.

serves 4
per serving 17.8g total fat (8.5g saturated fat); 1622kJ (388 cal); 39g carbohydrate; 18.6g protein; 9.1g fibre

150g oyster mushrooms, halved

200g fresh shiitake mushrooms, halved

200g swiss brown mushrooms, halved

2 large flat mushrooms (350g), chopped coarsely

300g vine-ripened tomatoes, chopped coarsely

1 small red onion (100g), sliced thinly

2 cloves garlic, sliced thinly

1 tablespoon olive oil

10g dried porcini mushrooms

1 cup (250ml) boiling water

2 cups (500ml) milk

1 cup (250ml) cold water

¾ cup (125g) polenta

20g butter

⅓ cup (35g) finely grated parmesan cheese

1 cup firmly packed fresh flat-leaf parsley leaves

½ cup coarsely chopped fresh chives

sumac-scented lamb and roast vegetable sandwich

PREPARATION TIME 20 MINUTES **COOKING TIME** 25 MINUTES

1 tablespoon lemon juice

1 tablespoon sumac

1 clove garlic, crushed

¼ cup (60ml) olive oil

400g lamb backstraps

1 small eggplant (230g), sliced thinly lengthways

1 small yellow capsicum (150g), sliced thickly

1 small red onion (100g), sliced thickly

2 small tomatoes (180g), sliced thickly

1 tablespoon balsamic vinegar

40g baby spinach leaves

⅓ cup loosely packed fresh flat-leaf parsley leaves

100g haloumi cheese, cut into four slices

4 ciabatta rolls (400g), halved

⅓ cup (80g) prepared hummus

1 Preheat oven to hot.
2 Combine juice, sumac, garlic and 1 tablespoon of the oil in medium bowl, add lamb; turn lamb to coat in marinade.
3 Combine eggplant, capsicum, onion, tomato and vinegar with remaining oil in large shallow baking dish. Roast vegetables, uncovered, in hot oven about 25 minutes or until tender. Place vegetables in medium bowl with spinach and parsley; toss gently to combine.
4 Meanwhile, cook lamb on heated oiled grill plate (or grill or barbecue) until cooked as desired. Cover lamb, stand 5 minutes; slice lamb thinly.
5 Cook cheese on same grill plate until browned both sides. Drain on absorbent paper. Toast rolls on same grill plate both sides.
6 Spread hummus on each roll half; top with lamb, vegetable mixture, cheese then other roll half.

serves 4
per serving 14.7g total fat (5.5g saturated fat); 2516kJ (605 cal); 82.8g carbohydrate; 26.3g protein; 2.6g fibre

RISOTTO 2WAYS

Risottos have become the heroes of many weeknight menus essentially because they can be as versatile as they are simple to prepare. They happily accept leftovers as ingredients, and can be chopped and changed to accommodate fussy diners. Each of these risotto recipes serves four people.

prawn and asparagus risotto

PREPARATION TIME 25 MINUTES **COOKING TIME** 45 MINUTES

500g uncooked medium king prawns

3 cups (750ml) chicken stock

3 cups (750ml) water

10g butter

1 tablespoon olive oil

1 small brown onion (80g), chopped finely

2 cups (400g) arborio rice

½ cup (125ml) dry sherry

10g butter, extra

2 teaspoons olive oil, extra

2 cloves garlic, crushed

500g asparagus, chopped coarsely

⅓ cup (25g) coarsely grated parmesan cheese

⅓ cup coarsely chopped fresh basil

1 Shell and devein prawns; chop prawn meat coarsely.
2 Place stock and the water in large saucepan; bring to a boil. Reduce heat; simmer, covered.
3 Meanwhile, heat butter and oil in large saucepan; cook onion, stirring, until soft. Add rice; stir rice to coat in onion mixture. Add sherry; cook, stirring, until liquid is almost evaporated.
4 Stir in 1 cup simmering stock mixture; cook, stirring, over low heat until liquid is absorbed. Continue adding stock mixture, in 1-cup batches, stirring, until absorbed after each addition. Total cooking time should be about 35 minutes or until rice is tender.
5 Heat extra butter and extra oil in medium frying pan; cook prawn meat and garlic, stirring, until prawn just changes colour.
6 Boil, steam or microwave asparagus until just tender; drain. Add asparagus, prawn mixture and cheese to risotto; cook, stirring, until cheese melts. Stir in basil.

per serving 14.7g total fat (5.5g saturated fat); 2516kJ (602 cal); 82.8g carbohydrate; 26.3g protein; 2.6g fibre

chicken, pea, sage and prosciutto risotto

PREPARATION TIME 20 MINUTES **COOKING TIME** 45 MINUTES

1 Place stock and the water in large saucepan; bring to a boil. Reduce heat; simmer, covered.
2 Heat butter and half of the oil in large saucepan; cook onion, stirring, until soft. Add rice; stir rice to coat in mixture. Add wine; cook, stirring, until liquid is almost evaporated.
3 Stir in 1 cup simmering stock mixture; cook, stirring, over low heat until liquid is absorbed. Continue adding stock mixture, in 1-cup batches, stirring, until absorbed after each addition. Total cooking time should be about 35 minutes or until rice is tender.
4 Meanwhile, heat remaining oil in medium frying pan; cook chicken, stirring, until cooked through. Add garlic; stir until fragrant. Stir chicken mixture and peas into risotto.
5 Cook prosciutto in same frying pan until crisp; drain on absorbent paper then break into coarse pieces. Stir sage and half of the prosciutto into risotto; sprinkle remaining prosciutto over individual risotto servings.

per serving 18.8g total fat (5.1g saturated fat); 2784kJ (666 cal); 84.1g carbohydrate; 24.5g protein; 3.9g fibre

3 cups (750ml) chicken stock

3 cups (750ml) water

10g butter

2 tablespoons olive oil

1 small brown onion (80g), chopped finely

2 cups (400g) arborio rice

½ cup (125ml) dry white wine

350g chicken breast fillets, chopped coarsely

2 cloves garlic, crushed

1½ cups (180g) frozen peas

6 slices prosciutto (90g)

2 tablespoons finely shredded fresh sage

asian stir-fried mussels

PREPARATION TIME 30 MINUTES **COOKING TIME** 10 MINUTES

1.5kg medium black mussels

1 tablespoon peanut oil

3cm piece fresh ginger (15g), sliced thinly

1 clove garlic, sliced thinly

2 shallots (50g), sliced thinly

2 fresh long red chillies, sliced thinly

½ teaspoon ground turmeric

¼ cup (60ml) kecap manis

¼ cup (60ml) fish stock

¼ cup (60ml) water

2 tablespoons lime juice

2 fresh kaffir lime leaves, shredded finely

1 cup firmly packed fresh coriander leaves

1 Scrub mussels; remove beards.
2 Heat oil in wok; stir-fry ginger, garlic, shallot, chilli and turmeric until mixture is fragrant. Add kecap manis, stock and the water; bring to a boil. Add mussels; return to a boil. Reduce heat; simmer, covered, about 5 minutes or until mussels open (discard any that do not).
3 Remove from heat, add remaining ingredients; toss gently to combine.

serves 4
per serving 6.1g total fat (1.2g saturated fat); 606kJ (145 cal); 12.2g carbohydrate; 10g protein; 1.2g fibre

TIP *Kecap manis sits alongside soy sauce in the cupboard these days: the two have quite dissimilar tastes and are called for in totally different kinds of recipes. An Indonesian sweet, thick soy sauce made with palm sugar, kecap manis can be used in marinades, dips, sauces and dressings, as well as a table condiment.*

thai beef salad

PREPARATION TIME 25 MINUTES (PLUS REFRIGERATION TIME)
COOKING TIME 10 MINUTES

One of everyone's favourites at the local Thai, our version of "yum nuah" is so easy to prepare and so delicious, you'll be making it at home rather than eating it out from now on.

1 Combine 2 tablespoons of the fish sauce and 1 tablespoon of the juice in medium bowl, add beef; toss beef to coat in marinade. Cover; refrigerate 3 hours or overnight.
2 Drain beef; discard marinade. Cook beef on heated oiled grill plate (or grill or barbecue) until cooked as desired. Cover, beef, stand 5 minutes; slice beef thinly.
3 Meanwhile, combine cucumber, chilli, onion, tomato and herbs in large bowl.
4 Place sugar, soy sauce, garlic, remaining fish sauce and remaining juice in screw-top jar; shake well. Add beef and dressing to salad; toss gently to combine.

serves 4
per serving 8.7g total fat (3.8g saturated fat); 986kJ (236 cal); 8.2g carbohydrate; 30.6g protein; 3.4g fibre

¼ cup (60ml) fish sauce

¼ cup (60ml) lime juice

500g beef rump steak

3 lebanese cucumbers (390g), seeded, sliced thinly

4 fresh small red thai chillies, sliced thinly

4 green onions, sliced thinly

250g cherry tomatoes, halved

¼ cup firmly packed fresh vietnamese mint leaves

½ cup firmly packed fresh coriander leaves

½ cup firmly packed fresh thai basil leaves

1 tablespoon grated palm sugar

2 teaspoons soy sauce

1 clove garlic, crushed

TIP *An intriguing thing about Thai food is how the simplicity of its ingredients conspires to create such a complex frisson of flavours. A little fish sauce, some lime juice and a few garlic cloves make magic in a Thai recipe, proving without doubt that the whole can be far, far more than the sum of its parts.*

1 cup (150g) plain flour

80g cold butter, chopped

1 egg yolk

2 tablespoons cold water

100g soft goat cheese

2 tablespoons coarsely chopped
fresh chives

CARAMELISED ONION

2 tablespoons olive oil

4 large brown onions (800g),
sliced thinly

⅓ cup (80ml) port

2 tablespoons red wine vinegar

2 tablespoons brown sugar

caramelised onion and goat cheese tartlets

PREPARATION TIME 25 MINUTES (PLUS REFRIGERATION TIME)
COOKING TIME 45 MINUTES

1 Blend or process flour and butter until mixture is crumbly. Add egg yolk and the water; process until ingredients come together. Enclose in plastic wrap; refrigerate 30 minutes.
2 Meanwhile, make caramelised onion.
3 Preheat oven to moderately hot. Grease four 10.5cm loose-based flan tins.
4 Divide pastry into four portions. Roll one portion of pastry between sheets of baking paper until large enough to line prepared tin. Lift pastry into tin; press into side, trim edge, prick base all over with fork. Repeat with remaining pastry.
5 Place tins on oven tray; cover pastry with baking paper, fill with dried beans or rice. Bake, uncovered, in moderately hot oven 10 minutes. Remove paper and beans carefully; bake in moderately hot oven about 5 minutes or until tartlet shells brown lightly.
6 Divide onion mixture and cheese among tartlets. Bake, uncovered, in moderately hot oven about 5 minutes or until heated through. Sprinkle tartlets with chives.

CARAMELISED ONION Heat oil in large frying pan; cook onion, stirring, until onion softens. Add port, vinegar and sugar; cook, stirring occasionally, about 25 minutes or until onion caramelises.

serves 4
per serving 31.5g total fat (15.2g saturated fat); 2165kJ (518 cal); 43.6g carbohydrate; 11g protein; 4g fibre

FRITTATA 2WAYS

Almost as perfect a package as the egg itself, a frittata can be cooked in the oven or on top of the stove and eaten hot or cold, served as an elegant light meal or as a hand-held snack... and be tailored according to your tastebuds' desire! Each of these frittata recipes makes four servings.

smoked salmon, caper and dill frittata

PREPARATION TIME 5 MINUTES
COOKING TIME 30 MINUTES

6 eggs

½ cup (125ml) cream

1 teaspoon finely grated lemon rind

1 small red onion (100g), sliced thinly

½ cup coarsely chopped fresh dill

2 tablespoons drained baby capers, rinsed

200g sliced smoked salmon

1 Preheat oven to moderate. Oil deep 20cm-square cake pan; line base and sides with baking paper.
2 Whisk eggs, cream and rind in medium bowl.
3 Combine onion, dill and capers in small bowl. Spread a third of the onion mixture in prepared pan; top with half of the salmon then pour half of the egg mixture over salmon. Place half of the remaining onion mixture and remaining salmon in pan. Sprinkle remaining onion mixture over salmon then pour in remaining egg mixture.
4 Cook, uncovered, in moderate oven about 30 minutes or until frittata is set; stand 5 minutes before cutting.

per serving 21.7g total fat (10.4g saturated fat); 1229kJ (294 cal); 2.8g carbohydrate; 22.5g protein; 0.5g fibre

TIP *The difference in an Italian frittata and a French omelette is more than just a matter of origin. A frittata has its filling content mixed in with the beaten eggs before cooking, while an omelette is traditionally folded over the filling in the pan. Frittatas can be served at room temperature, making them perfect for picnics or lunch boxes, while an omelette is eaten hot. They're both delicious, however, so... viva le difference!*

chorizo, gruyère and olive frittata

PREPARATION TIME 10 MINUTES **COOKING TIME** 35 MINUTES

1 Preheat oven to moderate. Lightly grease deep 20cm-square cake pan; line base and sides with baking paper.
2 Whisk eggs and cream together in small bowl.
3 Cook chorizo in small frying pan, stirring, about 5 minutes or until crisp. Drain on absorbent paper then place in prepared pan with tomato, olives and cheese. Pour egg mixture into pan.
4 Cook, uncovered, in moderate oven about 30 minutes or until frittata is set; stand 5 minutes before cutting.

per serving 46.1g total fat (22.4g saturated fat); 23624kJ (565 cal); 10.4g carbohydrate; 28.5g protein; 1.9g fibre

6 eggs

½ cup (125ml) cream

2 chorizo sausages (340g), sliced thinly

2 large egg tomatoes (180g), seeded, sliced thickly

100g seeded green olives, chopped coarsely

100g gruyère cheese, grated coarsely

MAINS

crisp-skinned ocean trout with bavette

PREPARATION TIME 10 MINUTES **COOKING TIME** 20 MINUTES

375g bavette

¼ cup (60ml) vegetable oil

¼ cup loosely packed fresh
sage leaves

¼ cup (50g) drained capers, rinsed

6 green onions, cut into
5cm lengths

4 ocean trout fillets (880g),
skin-on

⅓ cup (80ml) lemon juice

1 tablespoon sweet chilli sauce

2 cloves garlic, crushed

1 Cook pasta in large saucepan of boiling water, uncovered, until just tender.
2 Meanwhile, heat oil in large non-stick frying pan; shallow-fry sage, capers and onion, separately, until crisp.
3 Cook fish, skin-side up, on heated oiled grill plate (or grill or barbecue) until crisp both sides and cooked as desired.
4 Meanwhile, place drained pasta in large bowl with juice, chilli sauce, garlic and half of the sage, half of the capers and half of the onion; toss gently to combine. Divide pasta mixture among serving plates; top with fish, sprinkle with remaining sage, remaining capers and remaining onion.

serves 4
per serving 18.3g total fat (3g saturated fat); 2784kJ (666 cal); 70g carbohydrate; 53.3g protein; 5.5g fibre

TIP *Bavette is similar in appearance to tagliatelle; however, it's an all-wheat pasta containing no egg. The length and flatness of this noodle-like pasta contribute to making a little sauce go a long way... so it's perfect for this ocean trout recipe.*

chermoulla chicken with chickpea salad

PREPARATION TIME 25 MINUTES (PLUS STANDING TIME)
COOKING TIME 20 MINUTES

1 Place chickpeas in large bowl of cold water; stand overnight, drain. Rinse under cold water; drain. Cook chickpeas in medium saucepan of boiling water, uncovered, until just tender; drain. Rinse under cold water; drain.
2 Meanwhile, combine ingredients for chermoulla in large bowl; reserve half of the chermoulla for chickpea salad.
3 Place chicken in bowl with remaining half of the chermoulla; turn chicken to coat in chermoulla. Cook chicken, in batches, on heated oiled grill plate (or grill or barbecue) until cooked through. Cover to keep warm.
4 Place chickpeas in large bowl with capsicums, tomato, onion and remaining chermoulla; toss gently to combine. Serve chickpea salad with sliced chicken, drizzled with juice.

serves 4
per serving 21.6g total fat (4.6g saturated fat); 1994kJ (477 cal); 22.5g carbohydrate; 47.2g protein; 9g fibre

1 cup (200g) dried chickpeas

4 single chicken breast fillets (680g)

1 medium red capsicum (150g), chopped finely

1 medium green capsicum (150g), chopped finely

2 large egg tomatoes (180g), chopped finely

1 small white onion (80g), chopped finely

2 tablespoons lemon juice

CHERMOULLA

½ cup finely chopped fresh coriander

½ cup finely chopped fresh flat-leaf parsley

3 cloves garlic, crushed

2 tablespoons white wine vinegar

2 tablespoons lemon juice

1 teaspoon sweet paprika

½ teaspoon ground cumin

2 tablespoons olive oil

TIP *Chermoulla is a Moroccan blend of fresh and ground herbs and spices, including cumin, coriander and paprika, traditionally used for preserving or seasoning meat, poultry or fish. We used it as a quick flavouring for both the chicken and salad, to bring both elements of this recipe together.*

chicken green curry

PREPARATION TIME 40 MINUTES **COOKING TIME** 25 MINUTES

¼ cup (70g) green curry paste
(see recipe below)

3¼ cups (800ml) coconut milk

2 fresh kaffir lime leaves, torn

1 tablespoon peanut oil

1kg chicken thigh
fillets, quartered

2 tablespoons fish sauce

2 tablespoons lime juice

1 tablespoon grated palm sugar

100g green beans, trimmed,
chopped coarsely

2 small zucchini (300g),
chopped coarsely

⅓ cup loosely packed fresh thai
basil leaves

¼ cup coarsely chopped fresh
coriander

1 tablespoon fresh coriander
leaves

1 long green chilli, sliced thinly

2 green onions, sliced thinly

GREEN CURRY PASTE

1 teaspoon ground coriander

1 teaspoon ground cumin

8 long green chillies,
chopped coarsely

1 clove garlic, quartered

2 green onions, chopped coarsely

10cm stick (20g) thinly sliced
fresh lemon grass

1 fresh kaffir lime leaf,
sliced thinly

5g piece fresh galangal,
chopped finely

1 tablespoon coarsely chopped
coriander root and stem mixture

½ teaspoon shrimp paste

1 tablespoon peanut oil

*When removing the leaves from the coriander bunch,
keep the stems and roots as some of them are chopped
and used in the curry paste.*

*You need to use only a third of the curry paste in this
recipe. The rest can be frozen for later use.*

1 Make green curry paste.
2 Place ¼ cup of the paste in large saucepan; cook, stirring,
until fragrant. Add coconut milk and lime leaves; bring to
a boil. Reduce heat; simmer, stirring, 5 minutes.
3 Meanwhile, heat oil in large frying pan; cook chicken, in
batches, until just browned. Drain on absorbent paper.
4 Place chicken in pan with curry paste mixture; stir in fish
sauce, juice and sugar; simmer, covered, about 5 minutes or
until chicken is cooked through. Add beans, zucchini, basil
and chopped coriander; cook, stirring, until vegetables are
just tender.
5 Place curry in serving bowl; sprinkle with coriander leaves,
chilli and onion. Serve with steamed jasmine rice and extra
thinly sliced green chilli, if desired.

GREEN CURRY PASTE Dry-fry ground coriander and cumin
in small frying pan until fragrant. Blend or process spices
with chilli, garlic, onion, lemon grass, lime leaf, galangal,
coriander mixture and shrimp paste until mixture forms a
coarse paste. Add oil; process until mixture forms a smooth
paste. Measure ¼ cup of the paste for this recipe then freeze
the remainder (there will be about ½ cup), covered, for
future use.

serves 4
per serving 65.7g total fat (42.9g saturated fat); 3540kJ
(847 cal); 13.4g carbohydrate; 52.9g protein; 5.9g fibre

TIP *No longer just the province of the Chinese greengrocer, leafy Asian vegetables like choy sum, bok choy and gai larn can be found in almost every supermarket, on the menu in all kinds of restaurants... and in our vegie crispers at home. No wonder — they're fairly inexpensive, easy to prepare, full of nutrients and absolutely delicious.*

twice-cooked chicken with asian greens

PREPARATION TIME 45 MINUTES (PLUS STANDING AND REFRIGERATION TIME) **COOKING TIME** 1 HOUR

1 Combine the water, stock, wine, garlic, ginger and sesame oil in large saucepan; bring to a boil. Boil, uncovered, 10 minutes. Add chicken, reduce heat; simmer, uncovered, 15 minutes. Remove from heat, cover; stand chicken in stock 3 hours. Remove chicken; pat dry with absorbent paper. Reserve stock for another use.

2 Using sharp knife, halve chicken lengthways; cut halves crossways through the centre. Cut breasts from wings and thighs from legs to give you eight chicken pieces in total. Cut wings in half; cut breast and thighs into thirds. Place chicken pieces on tray; refrigerate, uncovered, 3 hours or overnight.

3 Make char siu dressing.

4 Heat peanut oil for deep-frying in wok; deep-fry chicken, in batches, until browned. Drain on absorbent paper.

5 Heat the 1 tablespoon of peanut oil in cleaned wok; stir-fry snow peas, choy sum and gai larn until just tender. Add 2 tablespoons of the dressing; stir-fry to combine.

6 Divide vegetables among serving plates; top with chicken, drizzle with remaining dressing, sprinkle with onion.

CHAR SIU DRESSING Stir garlic, ginger, sauces and sugar over heat in small saucepan until mixture comes to a boil. Remove from heat; stir in vinegar.

serves 4
per serving 47.4g total fat (12.5g saturated fat); 3081kJ (737 cal); 17.8g carbohydrate; 43.8g protein; 8.9g fibre

2.5 litres (10 cups) water

1 litre (4 cups) chicken stock

2 cups (500ml) chinese cooking wine

8 cloves garlic, crushed

10cm piece fresh ginger (50g), sliced thinly

1 teaspoon sesame oil

1.6kg chicken

peanut oil, for deep-frying

1 tablespoon peanut oil

150g snow peas, trimmed

500g choy sum, chopped coarsely

350g gai larn, chopped coarsely

2 green onions, sliced thinly

CHAR SIU DRESSING

2 cloves garlic, crushed

5cm piece fresh ginger (25g), grated finely

¼ cup (60ml) char siu sauce

2 tablespoons soy sauce

1 teaspoon white sugar

1 tablespoon rice vinegar

za'atar-rubbed lamb with chilli tabbouleh

PREPARATION TIME 30 MINUTES (PLUS REFRIGERATION TIME)
COOKING TIME 25 MINUTES

1 tablespoon sumac

1 tablespoon toasted
sesame seeds

1 teaspoon dried marjoram

1 teaspoon sweet paprika

2 teaspoons dried thyme

¼ cup (60ml) olive oil

2 lamb mini roasts (700g)

CHILLI TABBOULEH

3 medium tomatoes (450g)

½ cup (80g) burghul

1 small red onion (100g),
chopped finely

2 fresh long red chillies,
sliced thinly

5 cups coarsely chopped fresh
flat-leaf parsley

⅓ cup finely chopped fresh mint

½ cup (125ml) lemon juice

¼ cup (60ml) olive oil

1 Make chilli tabbouleh.
2 Preheat oven to moderately hot.
3 Combine sumac, sesame seeds, marjoram, paprika, thyme and oil in large bowl, add lamb; turn lamb to coat in za'atar rub.
4 Place lamb on oiled wire rack in large shallow baking dish; roast, uncovered, in moderately hot oven about 25 minutes or until cooked as desired. Cover lamb, stand 5 minutes; slice lamb thinly. Serve lamb with tabbouleh.

CHILLI TABBOULEH Chop tomatoes finely, retaining as much of the juice as possible. Place tomato and juice on top of burghul in small bowl, cover; refrigerate at least 2 hours or until burghul softens. Combine tomato burghul mixture in large bowl with remaining ingredients; toss gently to combine.

serves 4
per serving 45g total fat (11.1g saturated fat); 2675kJ (640 cal); 16.2g carbohydrate; 42.5g protein; 9.1g fibre

TIP *Za'atar, a blend of roasted dry spices, is easy to make, but a prepared mix of sesame seeds, marjoram, thyme and sumac can be purchased in Middle-Eastern food shops and delicatessens. Try it sprinkled on your morning toast that's been spread with softened fetta cheese or ricotta.*

japanese-style duck with cabbage and daikon salad

PREPARATION TIME 45 MINUTES (PLUS STANDING TIME)
COOKING TIME 1 HOUR 10 MINUTES

1 Place mushrooms in small heatproof bowl, cover with boiling water, stand 20 minutes; drain. Discard stems; slice caps thickly.

2 Combine mushrooms, the water, stock, sake, mirin, tamari, soy sauce, onion, garlic, ginger and sugar in stock pot. Add duck; bring to a boil. Reduce heat; simmer, uncovered, about 1 hour or until duck is cooked through. Remove from heat; stand duck in cooking liquid about 2 hours or until cool. Remove duck from cooking liquid; stand on wire rack 2 hours (discard cooking liquid). Cut duck into quarters.

3 Make cabbage and daikon salad.

4 Combine teriyaki and extra soy sauce in small bowl; brush over duck skin. Cook duck, skin-side down, on heated oiled grill plate (or grill or barbecue), 5 minutes. Turn duck skin-side up; brush with remaining teriyaki mixture. Cover; cook about 5 minutes or until duck is heated through. Serve duck with salad.

CABBAGE AND DAIKON SALAD Place carrot, daikon, cabbage, onion and chilli in medium bowl. Place miso, mirin, sake and sugar in small saucepan; stir over heat until sugar dissolves. Remove from heat; stir in vinegar and soy sauce. Add dressing to salad; toss gently to combine.

serves 4
per serving 94.8g total fat (28.7g saturated fat); 5488kJ (1313 cal); 48.6g carbohydrate; 44.2g protein; 4.6g fibre

10 dried shiitake mushrooms

3 litres (12 cups) water

1.5 litres (6 cups) chicken stock

1 cup (250ml) cooking sake

1 cup (250ml) mirin

¼ cup (60ml) tamari

½ cup (125ml) soy sauce

6 green onions, halved

3 cloves garlic, quartered

5cm piece fresh ginger (25g), unpeeled, chopped coarsely

½ cup (110g) firmly packed dark brown sugar

2kg duck

2 tablespoons teriyaki sauce

1 tablespoon soy sauce, extra

CABBAGE AND DAIKON SALAD

2 small carrots (140g), cut into matchsticks

½ small daikon (200g), halved lengthways, sliced thinly

½ small chinese cabbage (350g), shredded finely

3 green onions, chopped coarsely

1 fresh long red chilli, sliced thinly

2 tablespoons white miso

1 tablespoon mirin

1 tablespoon cooking sake

1 tablespoon white sugar

¼ cup (60ml) rice vinegar

1 teaspoon soy sauce

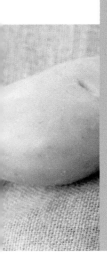

TIP *We used the creamy white, all-purpose sebago potato in this gratin but you can substitute it with desiree, spunta or any good baking potato, one that keeps its shape during cooking. Don't peel or slice the potatoes until you're ready to assemble the dish, and make sure you pat the slices dry with absorbent paper.*

veal scaloppine with potato fennel gratin

PREPARATION TIME 30 MINUTES **COOKING TIME** 1 HOUR 5 MINUTES

400g sebago potatoes

1 small fennel bulb (200g), sliced thinly

3 teaspoons plain flour

300ml cream

2 tablespoons milk

20g butter

⅓ cup (25g) coarsely grated parmesan cheese

½ cup (35g) stale breadcrumbs

2 tablespoons olive oil

8 veal schnitzels (800g)

2 tablespoons lemon juice

¼ cup (60ml) dry white wine

1 clove garlic, crushed

¾ cup (180ml) chicken stock

1 teaspoon dijon mustard

2 tablespoons drained baby capers, rinsed

¼ cup coarsely chopped fresh flat-leaf parsley

1 Preheat oven to moderate. Oil deep 1-litre (4-cup) baking dish.
2 Using sharp knife, mandoline or V-slicer, cut potatoes into very thin slices; pat dry with absorbent paper. Layer a third of the potato into prepared dish; top with half of the fennel. Continue layering remaining potato and fennel, finishing with potato.
3 Blend flour with a little of the cream in medium jug to form a smooth paste; stir in milk and remaining cream. Pour cream mixture over potato; dot with butter. Cover with foil; bake in moderate oven about 45 minutes or until vegetables are just tender. Remove foil, top with combined cheese and breadcrumbs; bake gratin, uncovered, about 20 minutes or until top is browned lightly.
4 During last 15 minutes of gratin cooking time, heat oil in large frying pan; cook veal, in batches, until cooked as desired. Cover to keep warm.
5 Add juice, wine and garlic to same pan; bring to a boil. Reduce heat; simmer, uncovered, until liquid reduced by half. Add stock and mustard; simmer, uncovered, 5 minutes. Remove from heat; stir in capers and parsley. Serve veal topped with sauce and accompanied by gratin.

serves 4
per serving 48.7g total fat (25.2g saturated fat); 3114kJ (745 cal); 22.9g carbohydrate; 51.7g protein; 2.9g fibre

roasted pork belly with plum sauce

PREPARATION TIME 20 MINUTES
COOKING TIME 1 HOUR 55 MINUTES

Take care that the pork rind doesn't get wet by the cooking liquid or the crackling will never crisp.

1 Preheat oven to moderate.
2 Place pork on board, rind-side up. Using sharp knife, score rind by making shallow cuts diagonally in both directions at 3cm intervals; rub combined salt and oil into cuts.
3 Combine the water, stock, soy sauce, wine, sugar, garlic, ginger, cinnamon, chilli, juice, cloves and fennel in large shallow baking dish. Place pork in dish, rind-side up; roast, uncovered, in moderate oven 1 hour 20 minutes. Increase oven temperature to very hot. Roast pork, uncovered, in very hot oven about 15 minutes or until crackling is crisp.
4 Remove pork from dish; cover to keep warm. Strain liquid in baking dish into medium saucepan, skim away surface fat; bring to a boil. Add plum, reduce heat; simmer, uncovered, about 15 minutes or until plum sauce thickens.
5 Meanwhile, make cucumber salad.
6 Serve thickly sliced pork with plum sauce and salad.

CUCUMBER SALAD Using vegetable peeler, cut cucumber lengthways into ribbons. Place cucumber in large bowl with remaining ingredients; toss gently to combine.

serves 4
per serving 51g total fat (16.2g saturated fat); 3010kJ (720 cal); 25.6g carbohydrate; 39.1g protein; 3.4g fibre

800g boned pork belly, rind-on

2 teaspoons salt

1 teaspoon olive oil

1 cup (250ml) water

1½ cups (375ml) chicken stock

2 tablespoons soy sauce

¼ cup (60ml) chinese cooking wine

¼ cup (55g) firmly packed brown sugar

2 cloves garlic, sliced thinly

3cm piece fresh ginger (15g), sliced thinly

1 cinnamon stick, crushed

1 teaspoon dried chilli flakes

⅓ cup (80ml) orange juice

6 whole cloves

1 teaspoon fennel seeds

4 plums (450g), cut into eight wedges

CUCUMBER SALAD

1 lebanese cucumber (130g)

1 long green chilli, sliced thinly

⅔ cup coarsely chopped fresh mint

1 tablespoon olive oil

1 tablespoon lemon juice

1 teaspoon caster sugar

2 tablespoons vegetable oil

1²/₃ cups (400ml) coconut milk

1 cup (250ml) coconut cream

2 cups (400g) jasmine rice

4 blue-eye fillets (800g), skinless

¹/₃ cup (15g) flaked
coconut, toasted

4 fresh kaffir lime leaves,
sliced thinly

SPICE PASTE

4 shallots (100g), quartered

50g piece galangal, quartered

½ teaspoon ground turmeric

½ teaspoon fennel seeds

1 teaspoon ground coriander

¼ cup (75g) madras curry paste

2 tablespoons lime juice

2 cloves garlic, quartered

4 fresh small red thai chillies

1 teaspoon caster sugar

malaysian fish curry

PREPARATION TIME 15 MINUTES **COOKING TIME** 30 MINUTES

1 Blend or process ingredients for spice paste until smooth.
2 Heat half of the oil in large frying pan; cook paste, stirring, over medium heat until fragrant. Add coconut milk and cream; bring to a boil. Reduce heat; simmer, uncovered, about 15 minutes or until curry sauce thickens slightly.
3 Meanwhile, cook rice in large saucepan of boiling water, uncovered, until tender; drain. Cover to keep warm.
4 Heat remaining oil in large frying pan; cook fish, uncovered, about 10 minutes or until cooked as desired.
5 Divide fish among shallow serving bowls; top with curry sauce, sprinkle with coconut and lime leaves. Serve rice in separate bowl; sprinkle curry with sliced chilli, if desired.

serves 4
per serving 56.2g total fat (34.9g saturated fat); 4468kJ (1069 cal); 89g carbohydrate; 52.4g protein; 6.7g fibre

TIP *Asian spice pastes are traditionally made with a mortar and pestle, as working the ingredients back and forth with the pestle breaks down their fibrous content, producing a paste that is thick, but not lumpy or stringy. For ease and speed, however, you can make the paste in a blender or food processor.*

kingfish with salsa verde and white bean puree

PREPARATION TIME 30 MINUTES **COOKING TIME** 25 MINUTES

1 Combine ingredients for salsa verde in small bowl.
2 Heat oil in medium saucepan; cook garlic and onion, stirring, until onion softens. Add beans and stock; bring to a boil. Reduce heat; simmer, uncovered, until almost all liquid has evaporated. Stir in cream; blend or process bean mixture until smooth.
3 Meanwhile, cook fish, skin-side down, in large heated oiled frying pan until cooked as desired.
4 Serve fish on white bean puree, topped with salsa verde.

serves 4
per serving 23.5g total fat (4.4g saturated fat); 1789kJ (428 cal); 7.4g carbohydrate; 46.9g protein; 5.6g fibre

1 tablespoon olive oil

1 clove garlic, crushed

1 medium brown onion (150g), chopped finely

3 x 400g cans white beans, rinsed, drained

1 cup (250ml) chicken stock

¼ cup (60ml) cream

4 kingfish fillets (800g), skin-on

SALSA VERDE

½ cup finely chopped fresh flat-leaf parsley

¼ cup finely chopped fresh mint

¼ cup finely chopped fresh dill

¼ cup finely chopped fresh chives

1 tablespoon wholegrain mustard

2 tablespoons lemon juice

2 tablespoons drained baby capers, rinsed, chopped finely

1 clove garlic, crushed

¼ cup (60ml) olive oil

TIP *We think salsa verde is just as good as pesto, and deserving of far more attention. It's not a spicy Mexican type salsa, but Italian, with a zesty, herbaceous, lemony flavour that goes well with fish and simple meat dishes. The herbs used in salsa verde can vary, with the single common denominator being flat-leaf parsley.*

moroccan lamb shanks with olive and almond couscous

PREPARATION TIME 20 MINUTES
COOKING TIME 2 HOURS 55 MINUTES

8 french-trimmed lamb shanks (1.6kg)

2 tablespoons plain flour

¼ cup (60ml) olive oil

2 medium brown onions (300g), chopped coarsely

3 cloves garlic, crushed

1 teaspoon ground cinnamon

2 teaspoons ground cumin

2 teaspoons ground coriander

1 cup (250ml) dry red wine

1 litre (4 cups) chicken stock

2 tablespoons honey

2 small kumara (500g), chopped coarsely

OLIVE AND ALMOND COUSCOUS

1½ cups (300g) couscous

1½ cups (375ml) boiling water

20g butter

2 tablespoons finely chopped preserved lemon

¾ cup (90g) seeded green olives, chopped coarsely

⅓ cup coarsely chopped fresh flat-leaf parsley

⅓ cup (45g) toasted slivered almonds

1 medium green capsicum (200g), chopped finely

1 Preheat oven to moderate.
2 Toss lamb in flour; shake away excess. Heat 2 tablespoons of the oil in large flameproof casserole dish; cook lamb, in batches, until browned all over, drain on absorbent paper.
3 Heat remaining oil in same dish; cook onion, garlic, cinnamon, cumin and coriander, stirring, until onion softens and mixture is fragrant. Add wine; bring to a boil. Reduce heat; simmer, uncovered, about 5 minutes or until liquid reduces by half.
4 Add stock and honey to same dish; bring to a boil. Return lamb to casserole dish; cook, covered, in moderate oven about 1 hour 30 minutes, turning shanks occasionally. Uncover dish, add kumara; cook, uncovered, about 50 minutes or until kumara is just tender and lamb is almost falling off the bone. Transfer lamb and kumara to platter; cover to keep warm.
5 Place dish with pan juices over high heat; bring to a boil. Boil, uncovered, about 15 minutes or until sauce thickens slightly.
6 Meanwhile, make olive and almond couscous.
7 Serve shanks with couscous.

OLIVE AND ALMOND COUSCOUS Combine couscous with the water and butter in large heatproof bowl, cover; stand about 5 minutes or until water is absorbed, fluffing with fork occasionally. Stir in remaining ingredients.

serves 4
per serving 38.1g total fat (11.5g saturated fat); 4339kJ (1038 cal); 98.4g carbohydrate; 65.3g protein; 5.8g fibre

TIP *Soak unshucked corn cobs in a pan of cold water for an hour or so. Pull back each cob's husk without removing it then remove the silk. Brush melted butter over the kernels then re-cover cob with the husk. Put corn directly on your hot barbecue grill for about 10 minutes, turning once. The result is delicious!*

mexican char-grilled scallops with corn salsa

PREPARATION TIME 25 MINUTES (PLUS REFRIGERATION TIME)
COOKING TIME 20 MINUTES

1 Combine scallops, garlic, juice and oil in large bowl. Cover; refrigerate 3 hours or overnight.
2 Place ingredients for lime dressing in screw-top jar; shake well.
3 Cook corn on heated oiled grill plate (or grill or barbecue) until browned lightly and just tender. Using sharp knife, cut corn kernels from cobs. Place corn kernels in large bowl with tomato, avocado, onion, capsicum, chilli, coriander and dressing; toss gently to combine.
4 Cook drained scallops, in batches, on same grill plate until browned lightly and cooked as desired. Cover to keep warm.
5 Using tongs, place tortillas, one at a time, briefly, on same grill plate to lightly brown both sides (work quickly as tortillas toughen if overcooked). Wrap tortillas in tea towel to keep warm.
6 Serve scallops with salsa, lime wedges and tortillas.

serves 4
per serving 24.1g total fat (4.4g saturated fat); 2416kJ (578 cal); 50.6g carbohydrate; 37.8g protein; 12.2g fibre

36 scallops (900g), roe removed

2 cloves garlic, crushed

2 tablespoons lime juice

1 tablespoon olive oil

2 corn cobs (800g), trimmed

200g grape tomatoes, halved

1 large avocado (320g), chopped coarsely

1 medium red onion (170g), chopped finely

1 medium green capsicum (200g), chopped finely

2 fresh small red thai chillies, chopped finely

¼ cup coarsely chopped fresh coriander

8 corn tortillas

2 limes, cut into wedges

LIME DRESSING

¼ cup (60ml) lime juice

½ teaspoon ground cumin

2 teaspoons olive oil

barbecued chilli prawns with fresh mango salad

PREPARATION TIME 25 MINUTES **COOKING TIME** 10 MINUTES

1kg uncooked large king prawns

½ teaspoon ground turmeric

1 teaspoon chilli powder

2 teaspoons sweet paprika

2 cloves garlic, crushed

MANGO SALAD

2 large mangoes (1.2kg), chopped coarsely

1 small red onion (100g), sliced thinly

1 fresh long red chilli, seeded, sliced thinly

1½ cups (120g) bean sprouts

½ cup coarsely chopped fresh coriander

2 teaspoons fish sauce

2 teaspoons grated palm sugar

2 tablespoons lime juice

1 tablespoon peanut oil

1 Place ingredients for mango salad in medium bowl; toss gently to combine.
2 Shell and devein prawns, leaving tails intact. Combine turmeric, chilli, paprika and garlic in large bowl, add prawns; toss prawns to coat in chilli mixture.
3 Cook prawns, in batches, on heated oiled grill plate (or grill or barbecue) until browned lightly. Serve prawns with salad.

serves 4
per serving 5.9g total fat (1g saturated fat); 1229kJ (294 cal); 30.3g carbohydrate; 29.5g protein; 5.1g fibre

TIP *While the best mango experience might be found standing at the sink eating a chilled juicy fruit in your hands, this sensual tropical food produces magic no matter how it's eaten: in salsas with grilled seafood, sliced with cold ham and turkey, or pureed in a smoothie, gelato or cocktail — all are deliciously heaven!*

grilled vegetables and basil tapenade pasta

PREPARATION TIME 20 MINUTES **COOKING TIME** 25 MINUTES

1 Blend or process ingredients for basil tapenade until smooth.
2 Cook eggplant, zucchini and tomatoes, in batches, on heated oiled grill plate (or grill or barbecue) until browned.
3 Meanwhile, cook pasta in large saucepan of boiling water, uncovered, until just tender; drain.
4 Place pasta in medium bowl with vegetables, tapenade and basil leaves; toss gently to combine.

serves 4
per serving 20.7g total fat (2.9g saturated fat); 25.4kJ (599 cal); 88.8g carbohydrate; 13.5g protein; 10.5g fibre

1 large eggplant (500g), sliced thickly

2 large zucchini (300g), sliced thickly

250g cherry tomatoes

375g tagliatelle

1 cup loosely packed fresh basil leaves

BASIL TAPENADE

2½ cups (300g) seeded black olives

2 tablespoons drained capers, rinsed

1 clove garlic, quartered

2 tablespoons lemon juice

¼ cup loosely packed fresh basil leaves

⅓ cup (80ml) olive oil

TIP *Making the tapenade using a mortar and pestle will give it a lovely thick, yet smooth, texture. Try stirring a spoonful of tapenade into a pasta sauce or vegetable soup, spreading it on a slice of bruschetta or canapé base, or thinning it with mayonnaise for a dip or lemon and olive oil to flavour a mixed salad.*

TIP *The blue cheeses of England, France and Italy - stilton, roquefort and gorgonzola, respectively - are the mould-ripened cheese copied by other countries when making savoury, aromatic, firm blue-vein cheeses. These are the best blues to cook with, as their distinctive flavour doesn't dissipate when introduced to heat.*

porterhouse steaks with blue cheese mash

PREPARATION TIME 30 MINUTES **COOKING TIME** 40 MINUTES

1 tablespoon olive oil

20g butter

2 large red onions (600g), sliced thinly

2 tablespoons brown sugar

2 tablespoons balsamic vinegar

4 porterhouse steaks (1kg)

½ cup (125ml) dry red wine

¾ cup (180ml) chicken stock

20g cold butter, chopped, extra

BLUE CHEESE MASH

1kg coliban potatoes, chopped coarsely

40g butter, softened

¾ cup (180ml) hot milk

100g firm blue cheese, crumbled

¼ cup coarsely chopped fresh chives

1 Heat oil and butter in large frying pan; cook onion, stirring, until onions softens. Add sugar and vinegar; cook, stirring occasionally, about 15 minutes or until onion caramelises. Cover to keep warm.
2 Meanwhile, make blue cheese mash.
3 Cook beef, in batches, in large heated lightly oiled frying pan until cooked as desired. Cover beef; stand 10 minutes.
4 Meanwhile, bring wine to a boil in same pan; boil, uncovered, until reduced by half. Add stock; return to a boil. Whisk in cold butter, piece by piece, until sauce is smooth.
5 Divide beef, onion and mash among serving plates; drizzle with sauce.

BLUE CHEESE MASH Boil, steam or microwave potato until tender, drain. Mash potato in large bowl with butter and milk until smooth; fold in cheese and chives. Cover to keep warm.

serves 4
per serving 54.1g total fat (28.1g saturated fat); 3958kJ (947 cal); 43.3g carbohydrate; 66.6g protein; 5.5g fibre

TIP *We are spoilt for choice when it comes to mushrooms. After the button, cup and flat varieties, the most readily available are enoki, swiss brown and oyster, which are the mushrooms we used here. Not only do they taste differently from one to the other, but each holds its shape well when cooked.*

roasted eye fillet with rösti and mushrooms

PREPARATION TIME 20 MINUTES **COOKING TIME** 45 MINUTES

1 Preheat oven to moderately hot.
2 Heat oil in large shallow flameproof baking dish; cook beef, uncovered, until browned all over. Roast, uncovered, in moderately hot oven about 35 minutes or until cooked as desired. Cover to keep warm.
3 Meanwhile, coarsely grate kumara and potatoes into large bowl. Using hands, squeeze out excess moisture from potato mixture; shape mixture into eight portions. Heat 10g of the butter and 1 teaspoon of the extra oil in medium non-stick frying pan; spread one portion of the potato mixture over base of pan, flatten with spatula to form a firm pancake-like rösti. Cook, uncovered, over medium heat until browned; invert rösti onto large plate then gently slide back into pan to cook other side. Drain on absorbent paper; cover to keep warm. Repeat process with remaining butter, oil and potato mixture.
4 Heat extra butter in same cleaned pan; cook mushrooms, stirring, until just tender. Add crème fraîche; bring to a boil. Reduce heat; simmer, stirring, until sauce thickens slightly. Remove from heat; stir in onion and parsley. Serve mushrooms with rösti and sliced beef.

serves 4
per serving 69.9g total fat (34.1g saturated fat); 4080kJ (976 cal); 34.4g carbohydrate; 54.2g protein; 8.4g fibre

2 tablespoons olive oil

800g beef eye fillet

1 large kumara (500g)

2 large russet burbank potatoes (600g)

80g butter

2 tablespoons olive oil, extra

30g butter, extra

200g swiss brown mushrooms, halved

200g enoki mushrooms, trimmed

150g oyster mushrooms, halved

200g crème fraîche

3 green onions, sliced thinly

⅓ cup firmly packed fresh flat-leaf parsley

lemon-pepper lamb with minted broad bean risoni

PREPARATION TIME 35 MINUTES (PLUS REFRIGERATION TIME)
COOKING TIME 20 MINUTES

1 tablespoon finely grated lemon rind

1 tablespoon cracked black pepper

2 teaspoons sea salt

1 clove garlic, sliced thinly

2 tablespoons olive oil

4 lamb backstraps (800g)

500g frozen broad beans

¾ cup (165g) risoni

4 green onions, sliced thinly

⅔ cup coarsely chopped fresh flat-leaf parsley

½ cup coarsely chopped fresh mint

2 tablespoons lemon juice

1 Combine rind, pepper, salt, garlic and half of the oil in large bowl, add lamb; turn lamb to coat in lemon-pepper mixture. Cover; refrigerate 1 hour.

2 Meanwhile, place broad beans in large heatproof bowl, cover with boiling water; stand 10 minutes. Drain beans; when cool enough to handle, peel grey outer shell from beans. Discard shells; reserve beans.

3 Cook risoni in large saucepan of boiling water until just tender; drain. Rinse under cold water; drain.

4 Meanwhile, heat remaining oil in large non-stick frying pan; cook lamb, uncovered, until cooked as desired. Cover lamb, stand 5 minutes; slice lamb thickly.

5 Cook onion, stirring, in same pan until just softened. Add risoni and beans; cook, stirring, until heated through. Remove from heat; stir in herbs and juice. Serve broad bean risoni with lamb.

serves 4
per serving 17.2g total fat (4.6g saturated fat); 2190kJ (524 cal); 37.4g carbohydrate; 53.6g protein; 10.4g fibre

TIP *A small rice-sized pasta, risoni is most often used in hearty soups, as is its near relative, the slightly larger orzo, which means "barley" in Italian. Both small pastas are also often used as a substitute for rice and other grains in casseroles and bakes.*

osso buco with caper gremolata

PREPARATION TIME 25 MINUTES
COOKING TIME 2 HOURS 45 MINUTES

1 Toss veal in flour; shake away excess. Heat 2 tablespoons of the oil in large flameproof casserole dish; cook veal, in batches, until browned all over.
2 Heat remaining oil in same dish; cook onion, garlic, celery and carrot, stirring, until vegetables soften. Stir in undrained tomatoes, tomato paste, wine, stock and thyme.
3 Return veal to dish, fitting pieces upright and tightly together in single layer; bring to a boil. Reduce heat; simmer, covered, 2 hours. Uncover; cook about 30 minutes or until veal is almost falling off the bone.
4 Combine ingredients for caper gremolata in small bowl.
5 Divide veal among serving plates; top with sauce, sprinkle with gremolata. Serve with soft polenta, if desired.

serves 4
per serving 19.9g total fat (4.4g saturated fat); 2240kJ (536 cal); 13.2g carbohydrate; 68.7g protein; 5.3g fibre

8 pieces veal osso buco (2kg)

2 tablespoons plain flour

¼ cup (60ml) olive oil

1 medium brown onion (150g), chopped coarsely

2 cloves garlic, crushed

3 trimmed celery stalks (300g), chopped coarsely

2 large carrots (360g), chopped coarsely

2 x 400g cans crushed tomatoes

2 tablespoons tomato paste

1 cup (250ml) dry white wine

1 cup (250ml) beef stock

3 sprigs fresh thyme

CAPER GREMOLATA

1 tablespoon finely grated lemon rind

⅓ cup finely chopped fresh flat-leaf parsley

2 cloves garlic, chopped finely

1 tablespoon drained capers, rinsed, chopped finely

TIP *A classic gremolata of finely chopped lemon rind, garlic and flat-leaf parsley adds panache to myriad dishes other than a traditional osso buco – stir a spoonful into homemade tomato and fennel soup, sprinkle a handful over a steamed whole fish, or try rolling a quarter cup of it inside a boned leg of lamb.*

TIP *Imported French lentils du puy enjoyed such a flurry of popularity a few years ago that we started growing our own version of these delicately nutty-tasting brown-green pulses — and they've taken off like a rocket. Look for them sold under the names of french green or matilda lentils.*

beetroot and lentil salad with grilled pork sausages

PREPARATION TIME 25 MINUTES **COOKING TIME** 50 MINUTES

1½ cups (350g) small brown lentils

2 sprigs fresh thyme

850g small beetroots, trimmed

1 tablespoon olive oil

1 large brown onion (200g), chopped finely

2 teaspoons yellow mustard seeds

2 teaspoons ground cumin

1 teaspoon ground coriander

½ cup (125ml) chicken stock

150g baby spinach leaves

8 thick pork sausages (960g)

THYME DRESSING

1 teaspoon fresh thyme

1 clove garlic, crushed

½ cup (125ml) red wine vinegar

¼ cup (60ml) olive oil

1 Place ingredients for thyme dressing in screw-top jar; shake well.
2 Cook lentils and thyme, uncovered, in large saucepan of boiling water until lentils are just tender; drain, discard thyme. Place lentils in large bowl with half of the dressing; toss gently to combine.
3 Meanwhile, discard any leaves and all but 2cm of the stalk from each beetroot. Boil, steam or microwave unpeeled beetroots until just tender; drain. When cool enough to handle, peel then quarter each beetroot; place in bowl with lentils.
4 Heat oil in large frying pan; cook onion, seeds and spices, stirring, until onion softens. Add stock; bring to a boil. Remove from heat; stir in spinach.
5 Place spinach mixture and remaining dressing in bowl with beetroot and lentil mixture; toss gently to combine.
6 Cook sausages in same cleaned pan until cooked through; serve sliced sausages with beetroot and lentil salad.

serves 4
per serving 73.7g total fat (24.5g saturated fat); 4623kJ (1106 cal); 58.7g carbohydrate; 55.5g protein; 22.6g fibre

vegetarian lasagne

PREPARATION TIME 40 MINUTES
COOKING TIME 1 HOUR 30 MINUTES

1 Quarter capsicums; discard seeds and membranes. Roast under grill or in very hot oven, skin-side up, until skin blisters and blackens. Cover capsicum pieces in plastic or paper for 5 minutes; peel away skin.
2 Reduce oven to moderately hot. Place eggplant in colander, sprinkle all over with salt; stand 20 minutes. Rinse eggplant under cold water; drain on absorbent paper.
3 Meanwhile, make white sauce.
4 Place eggplant, zucchini and kumara, in single layer, on oven trays; spray with oil. Roast, uncovered, in moderately hot oven about 20 minutes or until browned and tender.
5 Oil deep rectangular 2-litre (8-cup) ovenproof dish. Spread ⅔ cup of the pasta sauce into dish; top with a quarter of the lasagne sheets, ⅓ cup of the pasta sauce, eggplant and a third of the mozzarella. Layer cheese with another quarter of the lasagne sheets, ⅓ cup of the pasta sauce, capsicum, and another third of the mozzarella. Layer mozzarella with another quarter of the lasagne sheets, ⅓ cup of the pasta sauce, zucchini, kumara, remaining mozzarella, remaining lasagne sheets and remaining pasta sauce. Top with white sauce, sprinkle with parmesan.
6 Bake lasagne, uncovered, in moderately hot oven about 30 minutes or until browned lightly. Stand 10 minutes before serving.

WHITE SAUCE Heat butter in small saucepan; add flour, cook stirring, until mixture thickens and bubbles. Gradually stir in milk; stir until mixture boils and thickens. Remove from heat; stir in cheese.

serves 4
per serving 32.5g total fat (19g saturated fat); 3189kJ (763 cal); 82g carbohydrate; 37.5g protein; 9.9g fibre

3 medium red capsicums (600g)

1 medium eggplant (300g), sliced thinly

1 tablespoon coarse cooking salt

3 medium zucchini (360g), sliced thinly

1 medium kumara (400g), sliced thinly

cooking-oil spray

2 cups (500g) bottled tomato pasta sauce

250g instant lasagne sheets

2½ cups (250g) coarsely grated mozzarella cheese

⅓ cup (25g) coarsely grated parmesan cheese

WHITE SAUCE
40g butter

2 tablespoons plain flour

1¼ cups (310ml) milk

¼ cup (20g) coarsely grated parmesan cheese

DESSERTS

tiramisu

PREPARATION TIME 25 MINUTES (PLUS REFRIGERATION TIME)

2 tablespoons ground
espresso coffee

1 cup (250ml) boiling water

½ cup (125ml) marsala

250g packet savoiardi sponge
finger biscuits

300ml thickened cream

¼ cup (40g) icing sugar mixture

2 cups (500g) mascarpone
cheese

2 tablespoons marsala, extra

50g dark eating chocolate,
grated coarsely

1 Combine coffee and the boiling water in coffee plunger; stand 2 minutes before plunging. Combine coffee mixture and marsala in medium heatproof bowl; cool 10 minutes.
2 Place a third of the biscuits, in single layer, over base of deep 2-litre (8-cup) dish; drizzle with a third of the coffee mixture.
3 Beat cream and icing sugar in small bowl until soft peaks form; transfer to large bowl. Fold in combined cheese and extra marsala.
4 Spread a third of the cream mixture over biscuits in dish. Submerge half of the remaining biscuits, one at a time, in coffee mixture, taking care the biscuits do not become so soggy that they fall apart; place over cream layer. Top biscuit layer with half of the remaining cream mixture. Repeat process with remaining biscuits, coffee mixture and cream mixture; sprinkle with chocolate. Cover; refrigerate 3 hours or overnight.

serves 6
per serving 70.4g total fat (45.5g saturated fat); 3536kJ (846 cal); 42.9g carbohydrate; 6.7g protein; 1.4g fibre

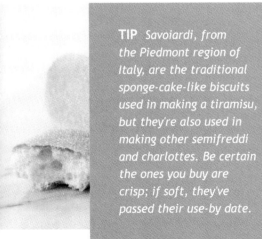

TIP *Savoiardi, from the Piedmont region of Italy, are the traditional sponge-cake-like biscuits used in making a tiramisu, but they're also used in making other semifreddi and charlottes. Be certain the ones you buy are crisp; if soft, they've passed their use-by date.*

raspberry bombe alaska

PREPARATION TIME 20 MINUTES (PLUS FREEZING AND COOLING TIME) **COOKING TIME** 10 MINUTES

1 Line four ¾-cup (180ml) moulds with plastic wrap. Press quarter of the ice-cream firmly up and around inside of each mould to form a cavity. Cover with foil; freeze about 2 hours or until firm.
2 Preheat oven to very hot.
3 Combine raspberries and caster sugar in small saucepan; stir gently over low heat about 5 minutes or until sugar dissolves. Cool 15 minutes.
4 Cut cake into four thick slices; cut one round from each quarter, each large enough to cover top of each mould.
5 Beat egg whites in small bowl with electric mixer until soft peaks form. Gradually add brown sugar, 1 tablespoon at a time, beating until sugar dissolves between additions. Fold in extract and cornflour.
6 Spoon a quarter of the raspberry sauce into one mould; turn mould onto one cake round on oven tray, peel away plastic wrap. Spread a quarter of the meringue mixture over cake to enclose bombe completely; repeat with remaining raspberry sauce, moulds, cake rounds and meringue mixture. Bake, uncovered, in very hot oven about 3 minutes or until browned lightly.

serves 4
per serving 28.4g total fat (15.7g saturated fat); 3143kJ (752 cal); 116.3g carbohydrate; 13.1g protein; 2.3g fibre

1½ litres vanilla ice-cream, softened slightly

1 cup (135g) frozen raspberries

1 tablespoon caster sugar

200g madiera cake

4 egg whites

1 cup (220g) firmly packed brown sugar

1 teaspoon vanilla extract

1 teaspoon cornflour

TIP *Packaged madeira cakes, found in nearly every supermarket, can be used as the base of baked Alaska or for turning into cake crumbs for rum balls. Similar to American pound cake or an English Victoria sponge, this sweet, buttery cake got its name in the early 1900s when it was eaten after dinner with a glass of Madeira wine.*

TIP *Figs have their origins in the long, hot summers of the eastern Mediterranean, and are at their best here from late January through March. A magnificent fruit, it's as exquisite eaten as an entree wrapped in thin strips of prosciutto as it is sprinkled with cinnamon and demerara sugar and grilled for dessert.*

clove panna cotta with fresh figs

PREPARATION TIME 20 MINUTES (PLUS COOLING AND REFRIGERATION TIME) **COOKING TIME** 10 MINUTES

1 teaspoon whole cloves

300ml thickened cream

⅔ cup (160ml) milk

2 teaspoons gelatine

2 tablespoons caster sugar

½ teaspoon vanilla extract

4 medium fresh figs (240g)

2 tablespoons honey

1 Grease four ½-cup (125ml) moulds.
2 Place cloves, cream and milk in small saucepan; stand 10 minutes. Sprinkle gelatine and sugar over cream mixture; stir over low heat, without boiling, until gelatine and sugar dissolve. Stir in extract. Strain into medium jug; cool to room temperature.
3 Divide mixture among prepared moulds, cover; refrigerate 3 hours or until set.
4 Quarter figs; stir honey in small saucepan until warm.
5 Turn panna cotta onto serving plates; serve with figs drizzled with honey.

serves 4
per serving 29.3g total fat (19.2g saturated fat); 1639kJ (392 cal); 29.1g carbohydrate; 5.1g protein; 1.3g fibre

TIP *Using the actual bean imparts the real taste of aromatic vanilla to a recipe. But since the beans aren't cheap, make them do double-duty; after the seeds are scraped out of one, place the empty vanilla pod in a jar then cover it with caster sugar. Keep sealed, in the fridge, for whenever you require a flavoured sugar.*

nougat semifreddo with orange and honey syrup

PREPARATION TIME 20 MINUTES (PLUS FREEZING TIME)
COOKING TIME 5 MINUTES

A traditional Italian dessert, semifreddo loosely translates as "a bit cold", and can refer to any partially frozen sweet served at the end of a meal.

1 Split vanilla bean in half lengthways; scrape seeds into small bowl, reserve pod for another use. Add yolks and sugar; beat with electric mixer until thick and creamy. Transfer mixture to large bowl.
2 Beat cream in small bowl with electric mixer until soft peaks form; gently fold cream into yolk mixture.
3 Beat egg whites in separate small bowl with electric mixer until soft peaks form. Gently fold half of the egg whites into cream mixture; fold in nougat, nuts, honey and remaining egg white. Transfer mixture to 14cm x 21cm loaf pan, cover with foil; freeze 3 hours or until just firm.
4 Make orange honey syrup.
5 Stand semifreddo at room temperature 10 minutes before serving with syrup.

ORANGE HONEY SYRUP Place ingredients in small saucepan; bring to a boil. Reduce heat; simmer, uncovered, 2 minutes.

serves 4
per serving 51.6g total fat (25.5g saturated fat); 3532kJ (845 cal); 87g carbohydrate; 13.3g protein; 2.2g fibre

1 vanilla bean

3 eggs, separated

⅓ cup (75g) caster sugar

1½ cups (375ml) thickened cream

200g nougat, chopped finely

½ cup (75g) coarsely chopped toasted shelled pistachios

1 tablespoon honey

ORANGE HONEY SYRUP

¼ cup (90g) honey

1 tablespoon finely grated orange rind

2 tablespoons orange juice

FRIANDS 2WAYS

In France, friands are better known as financiers, because they were originally baked in tiny gold-bar-shaped pans. No matter what size tin you use, however, these moreish little cakes are still worth their weight in mouth-watering gold!

pear and hazelnut friands

PREPARATION TIME 15 MINUTES **COOKING TIME** 20 MINUTES

6 egg whites

185g butter, melted

1 cup (100g) hazelnut meal

1½ cups (240g) icing sugar mixture

½ cup (75g) plain flour

1 small corella pear (100g)

12 shelled toasted hazelnuts (10g), skinned, halved

1 Preheat oven to moderately hot. Grease 12-hole (⅓-cup/80ml) muffin pan or 12 oval friand pans; stand on oven tray.

2 Place egg whites in medium bowl; whisk lightly with fork until combined. Add butter, meal, sugar and flour; using wooden spoon, stir until just combined.

3 Core pear; cut lengthways into 12 even slices.

4 Divide mixture among prepared pans; top each with 1 slice pear and 2 nut halves. Bake, uncovered, in moderately hot oven about 20 minutes. Stand friands in pans 5 minutes; turn, top-side up, onto wire rack to cool.

makes 12
per serving 18.4g total fat (8.6g saturated fat); 1166kJ (279 cal); 26g carbohydrate; 3.9g protein; 1.4g fibre

TIP *Eating a friand may be one of the joys of a cafe stop, but you'll find nothing difficult about making your own. And, should you wonder what to do with all those egg yolks, you can freeze them, singly in the compartments of an ice cube tray, for another time. Or you can make more yum at the same time you bake the friands... think of lemon curd, chocolate mousse or vanilla ice-cream!*

coffee friands

PREPARATION TIME 15 MINUTES **COOKING TIME** 20 MINUTES

1 Preheat oven to moderately hot. Grease 12 x ½-cup (125ml) rectangular or oval friand pans; stand on oven tray.
2 Place egg whites in medium bowl; whisk lightly with fork until combined. Dissolve coffee powder in the hot water, add to egg-white mixture.
3 Add butter, meal, sugar and flour to egg-white mixture; using wooden spoon, stir until just combined.
4 Divide mixture among prepared pans; top each friand with two coffee beans. Bake, uncovered, in moderately hot oven about 25 minutes. Stand friands in pans 5 minutes; turn, top-side up, onto wire rack to cool.

makes 12
per serving 17.8g total fat (8.6g saturated fat); 1133kJ (271 cal); 25.2g carbohydrate; 3.9g protein; 1.2g fibre

6 egg whites

2 teaspoons instant coffee powder

2 teaspoons hot water

185g butter, melted

1 cup (100g) hazelnut meal

1½ cups (240g) icing sugar mixture

½ cup (75g) plain flour

24 whole coffee beans

chocolate bread and butter pudding

PREPARATION TIME 20 MINUTES **COOKING TIME** 50 MINUTES

1½ cups (375ml) milk

2 cups (500ml) cream

⅓ cup (75g) caster sugar

1 vanilla bean

4 eggs

2 small brioche (200g), sliced thickly

100g dark eating chocolate, chopped coarsely

⅓ cup (40g) coarsely chopped toasted pecans

1 Preheat oven to moderate.
2 Combine milk, cream and sugar in small saucepan. Split vanilla bean in half lengthways; scrape seeds into pan then place pod in pan. Stir over heat until hot; strain into large heatproof jug, discard pod.
3 Whisk eggs in large bowl; whisking constantly, pour hot milk mixture into eggs.
4 Grease shallow 2-litre (8-cup) ovenproof dish; layer brioche, chocolate and nuts, overlapping brioche slightly, in dish. Pour hot milk mixture over brioche.
5 Place dish in large baking dish; add enough boiling water to come halfway up sides of dish. Bake, uncovered, in moderate oven about 45 minutes or until pudding sets. Remove pudding from baking dish; stand 5 minutes before serving.

serves 6
per serving 50.1g total fat (27.8g saturated fat); 2796kJ (669 cal); 45g carbohydrate; 12.6g protein; 1.4g fibre

TIP *Rich egg-and-butter brioche can be made in the shape of a loaf or roll, but the most recognisable variation is perhaps the "brioche a tete", 'a roll with a head', formed by placing a small ball of dough on top of a larger one. One of France's first regional specialities, the brioche of Normandy dates back to the early 1400s.*

poached nectarines with orange almond bread

PREPARATION TIME 25 MINUTES (PLUS REFRIGERATION AND COOLING TIME) **COOKING TIME** 1 HOUR 20 MINUTES

1 Make orange almond bread.
2 Combine the water, sugar, star anise and rind in medium saucepan, stir over medium heat until sugar dissolves; bring to a boil. Boil, uncovered, 2 minutes. Add nectarines, reduce heat; simmer, uncovered, 20 minutes. Cool nectarines 10 minutes in poaching liquid.
3 Using slotted spoon, transfer nectarines from pan to serving dishes; bring liquid in pan to a boil. Boil, uncovered, about 5 minutes or until syrup reduces to 1 cup; strain into small bowl.
4 Cool syrup to room temperature; pour ¼ cup of the syrup over nectarines in each dish; serve with yogurt and almond bread.

ORANGE ALMOND BREAD Preheat oven to moderate. Grease and line 8cm x 25cm bar cake pan. Beat egg whites in small bowl with electric mixer until soft peaks form. Gradually add sugar, 1 tablespoon at a time, beating until sugar dissolves between additions; transfer to medium bowl. Gently fold in flour, rind and nuts; spread into prepared pan. Bake, uncovered, in moderate oven about 30 minutes or until browned lightly; cool in pan. Wrap in foil; refrigerate 3 hours or overnight. Preheat oven to slow. Using serrated knife, cut bread into 3mm slices; place slices on baking-paper-lined oven trays. Bake, uncovered, in slow oven about 15 minutes or until crisp.

serves 4
per serving 20.6g total fat (3.3g saturated fat); 2867kJ (686 cal); 112.6g carbohydrate; 15.5g protein; 7.9g fibre

3 cups (750g) water
1 cup (220g) caster sugar
1 star anise
10cm strip orange rind
8 small nectarines (800g)
⅔ cup (190g) greek-style yogurt

ORANGE ALMOND BREAD

2 egg whites
⅓ cup (75g) caster sugar
¾ cup (110g) plain flour
1 teaspoon finely grated orange rind
¾ cup (120g) blanched almonds

TIP *This almond bread is our take on a classic biscotti recipe, those crisp biscuits that go so well with after-dinner coffee. In Italian, "bis" means twice and "cotto" means cooked, hence the name. Their purpose-built texture means that biscotti last well if kept airtight... not that there will be any left after you sample a few.*

TIP *Some people draw breath at the long cooking times, but the quince is worth the wait. That this yellow nondescript-looking fruit can, with a few hours' cooking, transform itself into a deep-pink delectable treat — no wonder its other name is "honey apple" — and many believe it to be THAT fruit found in the Garden of Eden.*

quince tarte tatin

PREPARATION TIME 20 MINUTES (PLUS REFRIGERATION TIME)
COOKING TIME 3 HOURS

4 medium quinces (1.2kg)

1 cup (220g) caster sugar

1 litre (4 cups) water

¼ cup (60ml) orange juice

1 teaspoon finely grated orange rind

40g butter

PASTRY

1 cup (150g) plain flour

¼ cup (40g) icing sugar mixture

100g butter, chopped

1 egg yolk

1 tablespoon cold water, approximately

1 Peel and core quinces; quarter lengthways.
2 Place quince in large saucepan with sugar, the water, juice and rind; bring to a boil. Reduce heat; simmer, covered, about 2½ hours or until quince is rosy in colour. Using slotted spoon, remove quinces from syrup; bring syrup to a boil. Boil, uncovered, until syrup reduces to ¾ cup. Stir in butter.
3 Meanwhile, make pastry.
4 Preheat oven to moderately hot. Line base of deep 22cm-round cake pan with baking paper.
5 Place quince, rounded-sides down, in prepared pan; pour syrup over quince.
6 Roll pastry between sheets of baking paper until large enough to line base of prepared pan. Lift pastry into pan, tucking pastry down side of pan. Bake, uncovered, in moderately hot oven about 30 minutes or until pastry is browned lightly. Cool 5 minutes; turn tart onto serving plate, serve with vanilla ice-cream, if desired.

PASTRY Blend or process flour, sugar and butter until crumbly. Add egg yolk and enough of the water to make the ingredients just come together. Shape dough into ball, enclose in plastic wrap; refrigerate 30 minutes.

serves 6
per serving 20.7g total fat (12.9g saturated fat); 2098kJ (502 cal); 77.5g carbohydrate; 4.1g protein; 11.3g fibre

TIP *Our flourless cake confirms that marrying hazelnuts and chocolate in a recipe is a match made in heaven. If you wish, you can roast, skin and process whole hazelnuts to make the meal. Similarly, you can dot the top of the finished cake with whole roasted nuts before you serve it, either warm or at room temperature.*

flourless chocolate hazelnut cake

PREPARATION TIME 20 MINUTES
COOKING TIME 1 HOUR (PLUS COOLING TIME)

1 Preheat oven to moderate. Grease deep 20cm-round cake pan; line base and side with baking paper.
2 Blend cocoa with the water in large bowl until smooth. Stir in chocolate, butter, sugar, meal and egg yolks.
3 Beat egg whites in small bowl with electric mixer until soft peaks form; fold into chocolate mixture in two batches.
4 Pour mixture into prepared pan; bake, uncovered, in moderate oven about 1 hour. Stand cake 15 minutes; turn onto wire rack, top-side up, to cool. Dust with sifted extra cocoa.

serves 8
per serving 31.8g total fat (14.9g saturated fat); 2090kJ (500 cal); 49.5g carbohydrate; 7.4g protein; 1.8g fibre

⅓ cup (35g) cocoa powder

⅓ cup (80ml) hot water

150g dark eating chocolate, melted

150g butter, melted

1⅓ cups (295g) firmly packed brown sugar

1 cup (100g) hazelnut meal

4 eggs, separated

1 tablespoon cocoa powder, extra

rhubarb and coconut cake

PREPARATION TIME 25 MINUTES
COOKING TIME 1 HOUR 30 MINUTES

1½ cups (225g) self-raising flour

1¼ cups (275g) caster sugar

1¼ cups (110g) desiccated coconut

125g butter, melted

3 eggs, beaten lightly

½ cup (125ml) milk

½ teaspoon vanilla extract

1 cup (110g) finely chopped rhubarb

5 trimmed rhubarb stalks (300g)

2 tablespoons demerara sugar

1 Preheat oven to slow. Grease 14cm x 21cm loaf pan; line base with baking paper.
2 Combine flour, caster sugar and coconut in medium bowl; stir in butter, eggs, milk and extract until combined.
3 Spread half of the cake mixture into prepared pan; sprinkle evenly with chopped rhubarb, spread remaining cake mixture over rhubarb.
4 Cut rhubarb stalks into 12cm lengths. Arrange rhubarb pieces over top of cake; sprinkle with demerara sugar. Bake, uncovered, in slow oven about 1 hour 30 minutes. Stand cake in pan 5 minutes; turn, top-side up, onto wire rack to cool.

serves 8
per serving 24.8g total fat (17.4g saturated fat); 2044kJ (489 cal); 61g carbohydrate; 7.5g protein; 4.7g fibre

TIP *You need about seven large stalks of rhubarb for this recipe. When you buy a bunch, cut off and discard all the leaves, as they are poisonous. The taste of rhubarb stalks themselves is enhanced by combining them with certain other flavours such as orange, strawberry or the vanilla used here, to name a few.*

pistachio and polenta cake with blood orange syrup

PREPARATION TIME 10 MINUTES
COOKING TIME 1 HOUR 15 MINUTES

1 Preheat oven to moderately slow. Grease deep 20cm-round cake pan; line base and side with baking paper.
2 Make blood orange syrup.
3 Place sour cream, butter, sugar, sifted flour and soda, polenta, rind and the water in large bowl; beat on low speed with electric mixer until just combined. Beat on medium speed until mixture changes to a slightly lighter colour. Stir in nuts.
4 Spread cake mixture into prepared pan; bake, uncovered, in moderately slow oven about 1 hour. Stand cake in pan 10 minutes; turn cake, top-side up, onto wire rack to cool. Serve cake warm or cold with strained blood orange syrup.

BLOOD ORANGE SYRUP Combine ingredients in small saucepan; bring to a boil, stirring. Reduce heat; simmer, uncovered, about 15 minutes or until syrup thickens. Cool to room temperature.

serves 12
per serving 15.2g total fat (7.6g saturated fat); 1714kJ (412 cal); 64.3g carbohydrate; 5.6g protein; 2.1g fibre

300g sour cream

125g butter, softened

1 cup (220g) caster sugar

2 cups (300g) self-raising flour

½ teaspoon bicarbonate of soda

⅔ cup (110g) polenta

1 teaspoon finely grated blood orange rind

¾ cup (180ml) water

⅔ cup (100g) toasted shelled pistachios

BLOOD ORANGE SYRUP

1 cup (250ml) blood orange juice

1 cup (220g) caster sugar

1 cinnamon stick

TIP *The blood orange, with its red-streaked, salmony-coloured flesh, is thought to have occurred in nature by accident in 17th-century Sicily. In season for all too short a time in winter, blood oranges have a sweet, non-acidic pulp and juice with a slight berry taste; even the skin is not as bitter as other citrus.*

glossary

BEAN SPROUTS also known as bean shoots; tender new growths of assorted beans and seeds germinated for consumption as sprouts.

beetroot also known as red beets; firm, round root vegetable. Can be eaten raw or grated in salads; boiled and sliced; or roasted then mashed like potatoes.

BICARBONATE OF SODA also known as baking soda.

BOK CHOY also known as bak choy, pak choi, chinese white cabbage or chinese chard. Has a fresh, mild mustard taste; use stems and leaves, stir-fry or braised. Baby bok choy, also known as pak kat farang or shanghai bok choy, is small and more tender than bok choy. Its mildly acrid, distinctively appealing taste has brought baby bok choy to the forefront of commonly used Asian greens.

BURGHUL also known as bulghur wheat; hulled steamed wheat kernels that, once dried, are crushed into various size grains. Not the same as cracked wheat. Used in Middle-Eastern dishes such as kibbeh and tabbouleh.

CHEESE
bocconcini from the diminutive of boccone meaning mouthful, is the term used for walnut-sized, baby mozzarella. A delicate, semi-soft, white cheese traditionally made in Italy from buffalo milk. Spoils rapidly so must be kept under refrigeration, in brine, for 1 or 2 days at most.
gruyere a swiss cheese having small holes and a nutty, slightly salty flavour.

haloumi a firm, cream-coloured sheep-milk cheese matured in brine; somewhat like a minty, salty fetta in flavour. Haloumi can be grilled or fried, briefly, without breaking down.
mascarpone a cultured product made in much the same way as yogurt. It's whitish to creamy yellow in colour, with a soft, creamy texture.

CHICKPEAS also called garbanzos, hummus or channa; an irregularly round, sandy-coloured legume used extensively in Mediterranean and Latin cooking.

CHILLI available in many different types and sizes. Use rubber gloves when seeding and chopping fresh chillies as they can burn your skin.
thai small, medium hot, and bright red in colour.

CHINESE BARBECUED DUCK this duck has a sweet-sticky coating made from soy sauce, sherry, five-spice and hoisin sauce. Available from Asian food stores.

CHINESE CABBAGE also known as peking or napa cabbage or wong bok. Elongated in shape with pale green, crinkly leaves. Can be shredded or chopped and eaten raw or braised, steamed or stir-fried.

CHORIZO a sausage of Spanish origin, made of coarsely ground pork and highly seasoned with garlic and chillies.

CHOY SUM also known as pakaukeo or flowering cabbage, a member of the bok choy family; easy to identify with its long stems, light green leaves and yellow flowers. Is eaten, stems and all, steamed or stir-fried.

CIABATTA in Italian, the word means slipper, which is the traditional shape of this popular crisp-crusted white bread.

CLOVES dried flower buds of a tropical tree; can be used whole or in ground form. Have a strong scent and taste so should be used minimally.

COCONUT
cream is obtained commercially from the first pressing of the coconut flesh alone, without the addition of water; the second pressing (less rich) is sold as the milk. Available in cans and cartons at supermarkets.
milk not the juice found inside the fruit, which is known as coconut water, but the diluted liquid from the second pressing from the white meat of a mature coconut. Available in cans and cartons at supermarkets.

CORNFLOUR also known as cornstarch; used as a thickening agent in cooking.

CUCUMBER, LEBANESE short, slender and thin-skinned; this variety is also known as the european or burpless cucumber.

CUMIN also known as zeera, available in ground or seed form; avialable from supermarkets.

DAIKON also known as giant white radish. The flesh is crisp, juicy and white; the skin can be creamy white or black. Refrigerate, wrapped in a plastic bag, up to a week.

EGGPLANT also known as aubergine; ranging in size from tiny to very large and in colour from pale green to deep purple, eggplant has an equally wide variety of flavours.

EGGS some recipes in this book call for raw or barely cooked eggs; exercise caution if there is a salmonella problem in your area.

FLOUR
plain an all-purpose flour, made from wheat.
self-raising plain flour sifted with baking powder in the proportion of 1 cup flour to 2 teaspoons baking powder.

GALANGAL also known as ka, a rhizome with a hot ginger-citrusy flavour; used similarly to ginger and garlic as a seasoning and as an ingredient. Sometimes known as thai, siamese or laos ginger, it also comes in a dried powdered form called laos. Fresh ginger can be substituted for fresh galangal, but the flavour will not be the same.

GINGER also known as green or root ginger; the thick gnarled root of a tropical plant. Can be kept, peeled, covered with dry sherry in a jar and refrigerated, or frozen in an airtight container.

HERBS use herbs in the proportion of one to four for fresh herbs; eg, 1 teaspoon dried herbs equals 4 teaspoons (1 tablespoon) chopped fresh herbs.
coriander also known as cilantro or chinese parsley; bright-green-leafed herb with a pungent flavour. Often stirred into or sprinkled over a dish just before serving for maximum impact.
flat-leaf parsley also known as continental parsley or Italian parsley.
thai basil has smaller leaves and purplish stems, it has a slight licorice or aniseed taste, and is one of the basic flavours that typify Thai cuisine.

thai mint also known as marsh mint; similar to spearmint. Its somewhat thick round leaves are usually used raw sprinkled over soups and salads. Substitute with equal parts mint and coriander.

vietnamese mint not a mint at all, but a pungent and peppery narrow-leafed member of the buckwheat family. It is a common ingredient in Thai foods, particularly soups, salads and stir-fries. Substitute with mint or basil.

KAFFIR LIME LEAVES glossy dark green leaves joined end to end to form a rounded hourglass shape. Sold fresh, dried or frozen, the dried leaves are less potent so double the number called for in a recipe if you substitute them for fresh leaves. A strip of fresh lime peel can be substituted for each kaffir lime leaf.

KUMARA Polynesian name of orange-fleshed sweet potato often confused with yam.

MARSALA a sweet fortified wine originally from Sicily.

MESCLUN is a salad mix of assorted young lettuce and other green leaves, including baby spinach, mizuna and curly endive.

MIRIN is a Japanese champagne-coloured cooking wine made of glutinous rice and alcohol expressly for cooking and should not be confused with sake.

MISO is usually termed red or white, although 'red' miso is dark brown in colour and 'white' is more the colour of weak tea. Miso is a paste made from cooked, mashed, salted and fermented soy beans, and it is a common ingredient in soups, sauces and dressings.

MIZUNA Japanese in origin; frizzy green salad leaf having a delicate mustard flavour.

MUSHROOMS
dried porcini the richest flavoured mushrooms, also known as cèpes. They are expensive but, due to their strong nutty flavour, only small amounts are required for most dishes. Must be rehydrated before use.

enoki long, thin, white mushrooms, with a delicate fruit flavour.

flat large, flat mushrooms with a rich earthy flavour, ideal for filling and barbecuing. They are sometimes misnamed field mushrooms which are wild mushrooms.

oyster also known as abalone; grey-white mushroom shaped like a fan. Prized for their smooth texture and subtle, oyster-like flavour.

shiitake when fresh are also known as chinese black, forest or golden oak mushrooms; although cultivated, have the earthiness and taste of wild mushrooms. Are large and meaty; often used as a substitute for meat in some Asian vegetarian dishes. When dried, they are known as donko or dried chinese mushrooms; rehydrate before use.

swiss brown light to dark brown mushrooms with full-bodied flavour also known as roman or cremini. Button or cap mushrooms can be substituted.

NOODLES
rice stick especially popular South-East Asian dried rice noodles. Come in different widths, but all should be soaked in hot water until soft.

rice vermicelli used throughout Asia in spring rolls and cold salads; similar to bean thread noodles, only they're longer and made with rice flour instead of mung bean starch.

NORI a type of dried seaweed used in Japanese cooking as a flavouring, garnish or for sushi. Sold in thin sheets.

ONIONS
green also known as scallion or (incorrectly) shallot; has a long, bright-green edible stalk.

red also known as spanish, red spanish or bermuda onion; a sweet-flavoured, large, purple-red onion.

PAPRIKA ground dried red capsicum, available sweet or hot.

PINE NUTS also known as pignoli; not, in fact, a nut but a small, cream-coloured kernel from pine cones.

POLENTA also known as cornmeal; a flour-like cereal made of dried corn (maize). Sold ground in several different textures; also the name of the dish made from it.

POMEGRANATE an apple-sized, hard and leathery deep-crimson red fruit grown for its ornamental qualities as much as for its tangy sweet-tart seeds and juice.

PROSCIUTTO cured, air-dried (unsmoked), pressed ham; usually sold thinly sliced. Available from most delicatessens.

ROCKET also known as arugula, rugula and rucola; a peppery-tasting green leaf that can be used similarly to baby spinach leaves, eaten raw in salad or used in cooking. Baby rocket leaves are both smaller and less peppery.

SAKE Japan's favourite rice wine, is used in cooking, marinating and in dipping sauces. If sake is unavailable, dry sherry, vermouth or brandy can be used as a substitute.

SAUCES
char siu a Chinese barbecue sauce made from sugar, water, salt, fermented soy bean paste, honey, soy sauce, malt syrup and spices. It can be found at most supermarkets.

tamari a thick, dark soy sauce made mainly from soy beans, without the wheat (used in standard soy sauce). It is used in dishes where the flavour of soy is important, such as dipping sauces and marinades.

SHALLOTS also called french shallots, golden shallots or eschalots; small, elongated, brown-skinned members of the onion family. Grows in tight clusters similar to garlic.

STAR ANISE a dried star-shaped pod whose seeds have an astringent aniseed flavour; used to flavour stocks and marinades.

TURMERIC also known as kamin, is a rhizome related to galangal and ginger, must be grated or pounded to release its somewhat acrid aroma and pungent flavour. Can be substituted with the more common dried powder (use 2 teaspoons of ground turmeric plus a teaspoon of sugar for every 20g of fresh turmeric called for in a recipe).

WATER CHESTNUTS resemble chestnuts in appearance; small brown tubers with a crisp, white, nutty-tasting flesh. Available in cans from supermarkets.

index

facts + figures

Wherever you live, you'll be able to use our recipes with the help of these easy-to-follow conversions. While these conversions are approximate only, the difference between an exact and the approximate conversion of various liquid and dry measures is minimal and will not affect your cooking results.

LIQUID MEASURES

METRIC	IMPERIAL
30ml	1 fluid oz
60ml	2 fluid oz
100ml	3 fluid oz
125ml	4 fluid oz
150ml	5 fluid oz (¼ pint/1 gill)
190ml	6 fluid oz
250ml	8 fluid oz
300ml	10 fluid oz (½ pint)
500ml	16 fluid oz
600ml	20 fluid oz (1 pint)
1000ml (1 litre)	1¾ pints

MEASURING EQUIPMENT

The difference between one country's measuring cups and another's is, at most, within a 2 or 3 teaspoon variance. (For the record, one Australian metric measuring cup holds approximately 250ml.) The most accurate way of measuring dry ingredients is to weigh them. When measuring liquids, use a clear glass or plastic jug with metric markings. (One Australian metric tablespoon holds 20ml; one Australian metric teaspoon holds 5ml.)

DRY MEASURES

METRIC	IMPERIAL
15g	½oz
30g	1oz
60g	2oz
90g	3oz
125g	4oz (¼lb)
155g	5oz
185g	6oz
220g	7oz
250g	8oz (½lb)
280g	9oz
315g	10oz
345g	11oz
375g	12oz (¾lb)
410g	13oz
440g	14oz
470g	15oz
500g	16oz (1lb)
750g	24oz (1½lb)
1kg	32oz (2lb)

HELPFUL MEASURES

METRIC	IMPERIAL
3mm	⅛in
6mm	¼in
1cm	½in
2cm	¾in
2.5cm	1in
5cm	2in
6cm	2½in
8cm	3in
10cm	4in
13cm	5in
15cm	6in
18cm	7in
20cm	8in
23cm	9in
25cm	10in
28cm	11in
30cm	12in (1ft)

HOW TO MEASURE

When using graduated metric measuring cups, shake dry ingredients loosely into the appropriate cup. Do not tap the cup on a bench or tightly pack the ingredients unless directed to do so. Level top of measuring cups and measuring spoons with a knife. When measuring liquids, place a clear glass or plastic jug with metric markings on a flat surface to check accuracy at eye level.

Note: North America, NZ and the UK use 15ml tablespoons. All cup and spoon measurements are level.

We use large eggs having an average weight of 60g.

OVEN TEMPERATURES

These oven temperatures are only a guide. Always check the manufacturer's manual.

	°C (CELSIUS)	°F (FAHRENHEIT)	GAS MARK
Very slow	120	250	½
Slow	140-150	275-300	1-2
Moderately slow	170	325	3
Moderate	180-190	350-375	4-5
Moderately hot	200	400	6
Hot	220-230	425-450	7-8
Very hot	240	475	9

ARE YOU MISSING SOME OF THE WORLD'S FAVOURITE COOKBOOKS?

The Australian Women's Weekly Cookbooks are available from bookshops, cookshops, supermarkets and other stores all over the world. You can also buy direct from the publisher, using the order form below.

TITLE	RRP	QTY	TITLE	RRP	QTY
Almost Vegetarian	£5.99		French Food, New	£5.99	
Asian, Meals in Minutes	£5.99		Get Real, Make a Meal	£5.99	
Babies & Toddlers Good Food	£5.99		Good Food Fast	£5.99	
Barbecue Meals In Minutes	£5.99		Great Beef Cookbook	£5.99	
Basic Cooking Class	£5.99		Great Chicken Cookbook	£5.99	
Beginners Cooking Class	£5.99		Great Lamb Cookbook	£5.99	
Beginners Simple Meals	£5.99		Greek Cooking Class	£5.99	
Beginners Thai	£5.99		Healthy Heart Cookbook	£5.99	
Best Ever Slimmers' Recipes	£5.99		Indian Cooking Class	£5.99	
Best Food	£5.99		Italian Cooking Class	£5.99	
Best Food Desserts	£5.99		Japanese Cooking Class	£5.99	
Best Food Mains	£5.99		Kids' Birthday Cakes	£5.99	
Big Book of Beautiful Biscuits	£5.99		Kids Cooking	£5.99	
Biscuits & Slices	£5.99		Lean Food	£5.99	
Cakes & Slices Cookbook	£5.99		Low-fat Feasts	£5.99	
Cakes Cooking Class	£5.99		Low-fat Food For Life	£5.99	
Caribbean Cooking	£5.99		Low-fat Meals in Minutes	£5.99	
Casseroles	£5.99		Main Course Salads	£5.99	
Celebration Cakes	£5.99		Meals in Minutes	£5.99	
Chicken Meals in Minutes	£5.99		Mediterranean Cookbook	£5.99	
Chinese Cooking Class	£5.99		Middle Eastern Cooking Class	£5.99	
Christmas Book	£5.99		Midweek Meals in Minutes	£5.99	
Christmas Cooking	£5.99		Muffins, Scones & Bread	£5.99	
Cocktails	£5.99		New Finger Food	£5.99	
Cooking for Crowds	£5.99		Pasta Cookbook	£5.99	
Cooking for Friends	£5.99		Pasta Meals in Minutes	£5.99	
Cooking For Two	£5.99		Potatoes	£5.99	
Creative Cooking on a Budget	£5.99		Quick Meals in Minutes	£5.99	
Detox (Sept 05)	£5.99		Quick-mix Biscuits & Slices	£5.99	
Dinner Beef	£5.99		Quick-mix Cakes	£5.99	
Dinner Lamb (Aug 05)	£5.99		Salads: Simple, Fast & Fresh	£5.99	
Dinner Seafood	£5.99		Saucery	£5.99	
Easy Australian Style	£5.99		Sensational Stir-Fries	£5.99	
Easy Curry	£5.99		Short-order Cook	£5.99	
Easy Spanish-Style	£5.99		Sweet Old Fashioned Favourites	£5.99	
Easy Vietnamese-Style	£5.99		Thai Cooking Class	£5.99	
Essential Barbecue	£5.99		Vegetarian Meals in Minutes	£5.99	
Essential Microwave	£5.99		Weekend Cook	£5.99	
Essential Soup	£5.99		Wicked Sweet Indulgences	£5.99	
Freezer, Meals from the	£5.99		Wok, Meals in Minutes	£5.99	
French Cooking Class	£5.99		**TOTAL COST:**	**£**	

NAME

ADDRESS

POSTCODE

DAYTIME PHONE

I ENCLOSE MY CHEQUE/MONEY ORDER FOR £

OR PLEASE CHARGE MY VISA, ACCESS OR MASTERCARD NUMBER

CARD HOLDER'S NAME

EXPIRY DATE

CARDHOLDER'S SIGNATURE

To order: Mail or fax — photocopy or complete the order form above, and send your credit card details or cheque payable to: Australian Consolidated Press (UK), Moulton Park Business Centre, Red House Road, Moulton Park, Northampton NN3 6AQ, phone (+44) (0) 1604 497531, fax (+44) (0) 1604 497533, e-mail books@acpuk.com
Non-UK residents: We accept the credit cards listed on the coupon, or cheques, drafts or International Money Orders payable in sterling and drawn on a UK bank. Credit card charges are at the exchange rate current at the time of payment.
Postage and packing: Within the UK, add £1.50 for one book or £3.00 for two books. There is no postal charge for orders of three or more books for delivery within the UK. For delivery outside the UK, please phone, fax or e-mail for a quote.
Offer ends 30.12.2005

Test Kitchen
Food director *Pamela Clark*
Food editor *Karen Hammial*
Assistant food editor *Amira Georgy*
Test Kitchen manager *Cathie Lonnie*
Home economists *Sammie Coryton,*
Nancy Duran, Nicole Jennings,
Elizabeth Macri, Christina Martignago,
Sharon Reeve, Susie Riggall, Kirrily Smith
Editorial coordinator *Rebecca Steyns*
Nutritional information *Laila Ibram*

ACP Books
Editorial director *Susan Tomnay*
Creative director *Hieu Chi Nguyen*
Senior editor *Wendy Bryant*
Designer *Hieu Chi Nguyen*
Studio manager *Caryl Wiggins*
Design assistant *Josii Do*
Editorial coordinator *Merryn Pearse*
Sales director *Brian Cearnes*
Publishing manager (rights & new projects)
 Jane Hazell
Marketing director *Nicole Pizanis*
Marketing manager *Katie Graham*
Brand manager *Renée Crea*
Sales and marketing coordinator *Gabrielle Botto*
Pre-press *Harry Palmer*
Production manager *Carol Currie*
Business manager *Seymour Cohen*
Business analyst *Martin Howes*
Chief executive officer *John Alexander*
Group publisher *Pat Ingram*
Publisher *Sue Wannan*
Editor-in-chief *Deborah Thomas*

Produced by ACP Books, Sydney.
Printed by Times Printers, Singapore.
Published by ACP Publishing Pty Limited,
54 Park St, Sydney; GPO Box 4088,
Sydney, NSW 2001.
Ph: (02) 9282 8618 Fax: (02) 9267 9438.
acpbooks@acp.com.au
www.acpbooks.com.au
To order books, phone 136 116.
Send recipe enquiries to:
recipeenquiries@acp.com.au
AUSTRALIA: Distributed by Network Services,
GPO Box 4088, Sydney, NSW 2001.
Ph: (02) 9282 8777 Fax: (02) 9264 3278.
UNITED KINGDOM: Distributed by Australian
Consolidated Press (UK), Moulton Park
Business Centre, Red House Rd,
Moulton Park, Northampton, NN3 6AQ.
Ph: (01604) 497531 Fax: (01604) 497533
acpukltd@aol.com
CANADA: Distributed by Whitecap Books Ltd,
351 Lynn Ave, North Vancouver, BC, V7J 2C4.
Ph: (604) 980 9852 Fax: (604) 980 8197
customerservice@whitecap.ca
www.whitecap.ca
NEW ZEALAND: Distributed by Netlink
Distribution Company, ACP Media Centre,
Cnr Fanshawe and Beaumont Streets,
Westhaven, Auckland.
PO Box 47906, Ponsonby, Auckland, NZ.
Ph: (09) 366 9966 ask@ndcnz.co.nz
SOUTH AFRICA: Distributed by PSD
Promotions, 30 Diesel Road, Isando,
Gauteng, Johannesburg. PO Box 1175,
Isando 1600, Gauteng Johannesburg.
Ph: (2711) 392 6065/6/7
Fax: (2711) 392 6079/80
orders@psdprom.co.za

Clark, Pamela.
The Australian Women's Weekly
New classics.

Includes index.
ISBN 1 86396 408 8
1. Cookery. I. Title.
II Title: Australian Women's Weekly.

641.5
© ACP Publishing Pty Limited 2005
ABN 18 053 273 546